CREATING GREAT ADS

ARVIND UPADHYAY

If it's a bright idea, that's good. If it's well executed, that's good too. But if it's a persuasive execution of a terrific idea . . . that's advertising —BOB KILLIAN

Advertising is the best way to communicate to the customers. Advertising helps informs the customers about the brands available in the market and the variety of products useful to them. Advertising is for everybody including kids, young and old. It is done using various media types, with different techniques and methods most suited.

Let us take a look on the main objectives and importance of advertising.

Objectives of Advertising

Four main Objectives of advertising are:

Trial

Continuity

Brand switch

Switching back

Let's take a look on these various types of objectives.

Trial: the companies which are in their introduction stage generally work for this objective. The trial objective is the one which involves convincing the customers to buy the new product introduced in the market. Here, the advertisers use flashy and attractive ads to make customers take a look on the products and purchase for trials.

Continuity: this objective is concerned about keeping the existing customers to stick on to the product. The advertisers here generally keep on bringing something new in the product and the advertisement so that the existing customers keep buying their products.

Brand switch: this objective is basically for those companies who want to attract the customers of the competitors. Here, the advertisers try to convince the customers to switch from the existing brand they are using to their product.

Switching back: this objective is for the companies who want their previous customers back, who have switched to their competitors. The advertisers use different ways to attract the customers back like discount sale, new advertise, some reworking done on packaging, etc.

Basically, advertising is a very artistic way of communicating with the customers. The main characteristics one should have to get on their objectives are great communication skills and very good convincing power.

Importance of Advertising

Advertising plays a very important role in today's age of competition. Advertising is one thing which has become a necessity for everybody in today's day to day life, be it the producer, the traders, or the customer. Advertising is an important part. Lets have a look on how and where is advertising important:

Advertising is important for the customers

Just imagine television or a newspaper or a radio channel without an advertisement! No, no one can any day imagine this. Advertising plays a very important role in customers life. Customers are the people who buy the product only after they are made aware of the products available in the market. If the product is not advertised, no customer will come to know what products are available and will not buy the product even if the product was for their benefit. One more thing is that advertising helps people find the best products for themselves, their kids, and their family. When they come to know about the range of products, they are able to compare the products and buy so that they get what they desire after spending their valuable money. Thus, advertising is important for the customers.

Advertising is important for the seller and companies producing the products

Yes, advertising plays very important role for the producers and the sellers of the products, because

Advertising helps increasing sales

Advertising helps producers or the companies to know their competitors and plan accordingly to meet up the level of competition.

If any company wants to introduce or launch a new product in the market, advertising will make a ground for the product. Advertising helps making people aware of the new product so that the consumers come and try the product.

Advertising helps creating goodwill for the company and gains customer loyalty after reaching a mature age.

The demand for the product keeps on coming with the help of advertising and demand and supply become a never ending process.

Advertising is important for the society

Advertising helps educating people. There are some social issues also which advertising deals with like child labour, liquor consumption, girl child killing, smoking, family planning education, etc. thus, advertising plays a very important role in society.

Contents

Foreword

This book is a step-by-step guide to the creation or supervision of the most widely used advertising and promotional activities. Four kinds of audiences will find it particularly helpful: 1. The business, corporation, or organization that must do its own advertising and promotion. 2. Persons newly appointed or promoted to positions in advertising, promotion, marketing, or marketing services with little or no experience in those fields. 3. Managers with supervisory responsibility for advertising and promotion. 4. Adult education and in-house training directors who find traditional textbooks unsatisfactory for their needs. The book works equally well as a blueprint for the do-it-yourselfer, amateur or professional, or as a checklist for managers and supervisors. It is not a complete course in advertising. Each chapter covers a specific type of activity or project and is complete in itself. It focuses on just those things you must know and do to accomplish that specific objective—produce an ad, prepare a catalog, supervise a television commercial, and so on. Ordinary English is used as much as possible. When technical terms are introduced, they are defined immediately, in context. Like every other profession, advertising has its own language, and certain "ordinary" words can prove confusing to the uninitiated. ("Light" for "short" in advertising copy was my first such experience.) ADVERTISING AND PROMOTION Because "advertising" and "promotion" are often used interchangeably, even by professionals, some definitions may be helpful. In ordinary use, "promotion" is everything that is done to help sell a product or service in every step of the sales chain, from the presentation materials a salesperson uses during a sales call to the television commercial or newspaper advertisement that tries to get the customer to think favorably about what is being advertised. Technically speaking, however, "advertising" is responsible for "space" or "print"—that is, newspaper and magazine ads, Internet advertising, radio and television commercials, and direct mail and other "direct response" activities, plus catalogs and billboards. "Promotion" is responsible for everything else in this area except public relations and publicity. These last two may be assigned to an independent department or to either advertising or promotion, depending on the make-up of the company or organization. Because job titles and department designations are quite arbitrary, a detailed job description is highly desirable to avoid turf battles when more than one person or department does any of the above. Throughout this book, you will find "insights" that are meant to be both aids to memory and actual guidelines to action. Since many of them are applicable to more than one type of project, browse through these pages and read them all, even if the help and information you need are contained in a single chapter.

brand asset audit

we give a lot of weight to the use (and occasional misuse) of a name. Investigating the practical limits of line extensions, for example, forces you to distinguish between those new product efforts that reinvest brand equity, versus those that dilute it. In #1 on your Scorecard, give your brand anywhere from 0 to 5 points for the salesmanship built into the meaning of the name. Add from 0 to 10 points for its top-of-mind consumer awareness, a fair measure of the value of your prior investment in the brand's reputation. 2. Packaging Packaging is the ultimate final dialog with the consumer. It must call attention to itself, set the product apart from the category and other products in its own line. We don't know why packaging is so often regarded as separate from the selling process, a stepchild in the marketing family. Think of packaging and POP (Point of Purchase) as brand assets to be invested in and deployed like other managed assets. That will help focus on how important they are to the final sale. A family of packages can reassure consumers by projecting a persuasive brand personality and value-added consistency. At their most effective, packages can jump off the shelf and close the sale. (Note: Be creatively flexible here. If you're a service business, your "packaging" might be your selling tools, brochures, truck signs, whatever you use to speak to your customers. If you're a retailer, it's you store front and store atmosphere.) On your Scorecard, give your brand from 0 to 10 points for packaging and POP strengths. If you have a strong retail presence compared to your competitors, but not one that can be compared to the best of the best, don't give yourself more than 5. 3. Reach and Frequency When most people think of advertising effectiveness, they tend to think in terms of an ad budget. So some are deluded into believing that if we spend twice as much on our advertising, we will get twice the results. This was never true, and it is getting even less true every year. In an age where niche markets are proliferating and mass markets are mostly myth, it is very helpful to think of reach, frequency, and ad content as related but separate assets in your advertising portfolio. INSIGHT 4 The function of branding is to make it difficult and expensive for competitors to try to enter or compete in your market. Successful branding makes that practically impossible. Think of Bayer™ aspirin, Rand McNally's road atlases, Adobe PhotoShop. Others may sell in their markets, but only as fringe products. "Branding" defined by Dr. Rolf Weil, president emeritus and emeritus professor of finance, Roosevelt University, Chicago. 4 Branding and Your Brand Asset Assessment The New Importance of Reach With so many new marketing tools available to target specific audience segments, reach has become relatively more important than frequency. Niche marketing has created efficient new ways to get to specific consumer affinity groups and increasingly accurate psychographic slices of the almost-extinct mass audience. (Remember when there were general-interest magazines?) Frequency still is basically deploying money against markets, boxcar numbers flexing budgetary muscle. Market segmentation strategies can, however, deliver more leveraged results with equal frequency but (relatively) smaller budgets. Give yourself 0 to 10 points for smart segmenting. Then record 1, 2, or 3 for Shareof-Voice media spending: (1) below, (2) the same, or (3) above the spending level of competitors. 4. Ad Content The greatest leverage of advertising is in its creativity. A great ad can be, and often is, 10 times more effective than a mediocre one. It's possible, for example, to cut a media budget by 25 percent and know that you will lose roughly 25 percent of your effectiveness. But if you cut advertising production costs by 25 percent, you can't possibly know the impact. You might lose up to 90 percent of your effectiveness. Invest in Production Values We are not talking about throwing money around. It's true that dazzling production values can't rescue a nonidea. But it's also true that if, say, a TV spot has poor camera work, cheesy lighting, and an awkward, overly loud spokesman who would never be hired as a spokesperson for anybody else (you know, that local used car dealer in your market,) it can turn off an audience's receptors to even the strongest ideas. Even on radio, you can tell the difference between a national spot and a homemade local spot in the first few seconds—the false bargain of amateurish production values strikes again. Think of media spending as an unleveraged investment and ad content as highly leveraged. You will be less tempted to steal budget from the creative process to buy a few more spots in Lubbock. Candidly, score 0 to 10 points for what your ads say, plus

0 to 10 for how memorably and unexpectedly they say it. Then multiply that total by the Share-of-Voice score you gave yourself above. This is the single biggest score you'll get, because these assets are the biggest equity builders. It stands to reason: more leverage more importance more points. 5. Promotion Can promotion kill brand equity? Yes! Can promotions build brand equity? Yes, if one sees to it that the promotional activities enhance and reinforce the basic brand image. In other words, don't needlessly, blindly switch on a marketing autopilot, drop millions of high-value coupons, and call it a plan. To put it bluntly, sometimes FSI (Free-Standing Insert) stands for Failed to Search for Ideas Score 0 to 5 for a strategically sound promotion policy. Then subtract one point for every coupon promotion in the last 12 months. Range −12 to 5. 6. Consistency There are two kinds of consistency, and both are important for brands: consistency from year to year and consistency across all communications vehicles. Long-Term Consistency If your brand changes its personality every few years, it runs the risk of having no image at all. (What does Canada Dry stand for, anyway? How is a Plymouth different from a Dodge?) The Marlboro Man, on the other (tattooed) hand, suffers from no such confusion after five decades of consistent messaging, building to market dominance. Usually, two or three years into any brand-building campaign, a firm grip is needed to keep the agents of change-for-the-sake-of-change on a short leash. Just because they are tired of doing "the same old thing," doesn't mean it's penetrated into the heads and hearts of your target audience. Integrated Consistency The second kind of inconsistency that erodes brand equity is advertising, promotion, packaging, and public relations people who aren't reading from the same sheet of music. They each pursue their own vision, losing the single focus that successful branding demands and rewards. Score 0 to 10 for across-the-disciplines consistency, and 0 to 5 for across-the-years consistency. 7. Distribution The Consumer Products Problem In the conventional view, the single greatest problem for most consumer products brand holders is to get, hold, or expand retail shelf/ floor space. So the conventional (that is, easiest) solution is to "buy" the distribution. Buying Distribution Pay the slotting fees, display allowances, baksheesh, and listing fees to get the shelf space, then discount like crazy to keep your facings. Run an avalanche of coupons and rebates and similar margin-reducing activities to keep the inventory turning. That makes the retailer (not to mention the coupon delivery system) happy and prosperous. For many smart marketers, however, establishing a retail presence by

pushing with big trade deals and pulling with big coupons can be prohibitively unprofitable (and not altogether consistent with developing a brand). There are alternatives, such as smarter advertising, publicity, word of mouth, and the many aspects of promotion detailed throughout this how-to-book.

Score 0 to 6 for breadth of distribution (are you in all the geography you want?), plus 0 to 6 for the depth and cost of that distribution. (Are you overspending to maintain marginal regions? Channels? Markets? Customers?) 8. Newsworthiness Being in tune with the times offers lots of opportunities for "unpaid advertising."1 Clearly defined, strategically oriented public relations can be a powerful tool. They are assets that can induce trial, enhance brand image, and build brand equity, if it is consistent with your other messages. Do remember, however, that such unpaid advertising takes just as much skill to produce and place as the paid version! As in item no. 4, "Ad Content," it's the production that's critical, so budget your PR accordingly. Give yourself 0 to 5 points for how well you've exploited this brand asset. 9. Likeability Yes, likeability matters! And yes, it's measurable. If your communications (and therefore your brand) are likeable, then people will welcome your message. It's a fundamental truth: People buy from people (read: brands) they like. In consumer buying, there are no rational purchases. None. Give yourself up to 5 points for a refreshing brand "attitude." 10. Trade Support Leverage over competitors is the best result of enthusiastic trade support. For many brand holders, of course, that leverage can be enormous: In some industries, trade support can be life or death. Remember, in today's environment, you can achieve your goals only by making your trade network believe that you are helping them achieve theirs. Every sales force worth its salt cultivates relationship sales. Score 0 to 5 points for how your brand is supported (versus competitors) by the trade. 11. Sales Force You'd think that the scores you recorded for distribution would tell you all you need to know about your sales force. That is usually true, but any major change in a selling organization brings a dynamic to established distribution. Adding reps, changing sales management, or altering compensation programs—really, any substantial change—can weaken the strongest distribution or (conversely) pay big dividends. Should you plan such a change, test its outcome—on a regional basis, if possible. Testing permits you to reverse course before an impending disaster.

12. User Profile Certain user groups and market segments carry more significance and impact than others. Distinguish between high-index users (that's research-speak for the delightful 10 percent of your customers who buy 60 percent of your product) and merely high-potential users. For example, people with developing or changeable brand images are highly important. This translates in many cases into pursuit of the young, in hopes of securing a long-term predisposition toward a brand. If it works, when it works, the benefits can roll on for decades. Consider Honda. They pursued and nurtured a relationship with a whole generation of consumers and continued to fine-tune the product line to meet their changing needs. Beer marketers, too, know the value of a lifetime customer. Of 100 people loyal to a beer brand at age 21, 50 will still be loyal to that brand at age 30. On the other hand, narrow appeals mean narrowing markets. People who buy fur coats, Cadillacs, and shelf liner paper are dropping out faster than they're being replaced. This is not, however, irreversible. Whole categories (like gourmet coffee) have been rejuvenated by young trendsetters. Add 0 to 5 points to your score for having enough good research to know your user intimately. 13. Product Performance What You Get Is What You See It almost goes without saying that product performance is a key factor in a buyer's decision to repurchase. If the world were rational, the objective realities of product performance would generate trial, too. The key factor in a consumer's decision to try a product in the first place, however, is its perceived product performance. A CASE HISTORY Britannica Films hoped to sell a fire prevention film, produced for elementary schools, to municipal fire departments for their community outreach programs. To sweeten the offer, they tested the choice of a free popcorn popper or a set of topquality steak knives with each film. The result was immediate outrage! How dare Britannica assume a fire department would purchase a public safety film just to get something else for free! The subsequent nonpremium mailing was a huge success.2 8 Branding and Your Brand Asset Assessment .

Although it's up to you to maximize actual product performance, many different components of brand image influence consumers' perceptions of anticipated performance. That's a shared responsibility of advertising, promotions, packaging, POP—everything that "talks" to consumers. Score 0 to 5 for actual performance; add 0 to 5 for consumer perceptions of performance. 14. Repurchasing Frequency of use equals frequency of brand-affirming (or brand-switching) decisions. That's a key equation, because it helps explain why loyalties grow stronger to Snickers candy bars (bought three days a week) than to oatmeal (bought once every first snowfall.) It also helps you know how many trials you have to induce to conquer competitive users. You can never know too much about purchaser behavior. Do repurchase patterns change by time of day, time of year, retail environment, competitive pressure, or promotional activity? Can these behaviors be altered? What are your use-up rates? Do users take themselves out of the market for a considerable time with each purchase? Who Deserves Loyalty from Whom Too many marketers bask in the glow of so-called brand loyalty, which has the unintended consequence of taking good customers for granted. Nobody should count on the continued (blind) loyalty of people who have chosen a brand in the past. Brand owners should be loyal to their customers, not the other way around. Consumers will buy and rebuy only those brands that continue to live up to their perceptions of added value How well have you planned and exploited ways to promote additional uses/occasions, which tend to increase the velocity of repurchase? Score 0 to 5. 15. Actionable Research In an age of computerized databases, and number-crunching machines of awesome speed, there is little or no problem with the quantity of information available to us. Indeed, the problem is the opposite. It's analysis paralysis. From Data to Decisions The key is how to turn data into decisions. The key to the key (to murder our metaphor) is to recognize and use actionable research. Do your findings lead to action or just to filling PowerPoint slides? Can you make the leap from raw tabs to real insight? Can you learn how to use your brand assets more creatively, more unexpectedly? If not, save the research money. The ongoing fascination with focus groups (and concurrent neglect of quantitative studies) has had unfortunate side effects. Some marketers suffer because they broke rule one: They tried to project quantitative results from qualitative research. We call it the "But-that's-what-the-woman-in-Walla-Walla-said" syndrome. The absurd number of new product offerings is a monument to this kind of wishful thinking. One of your most valuable functions is to act as if an alien visitor arrived from another marketing planet. Question every old assumption, all research, any comfortable ritual. If your research is aging (or missing), or it's been a while since your corporate assumptions have been challenged, it's time to restate all your questions and question all your answers. Subtract 5 points for wasting money on useless research, score 0 points for no research, and give yourself up to 5 for actionable results that make you say "Aha!" 16. Value In a rational world, price would equal value. (Of course, in a rational world, there'd be no civil wars or salad shooters. But we digress.) Price is just one element in the complex, nonrational perception tug-of-war within consumer buying decisions. Value equals perceived quality, divided by actual price. Perceived quality, of course, is what you hope to establish with your other assets. Pricing decisions, insofar as a brand holder can actually control (or even influence) them, have to be handled with much more skill and attention then simply throwing coupons or rebates at potential buyers. They require continuing attention to each and every one of the first 15 points in your Brand Asset Assessment. That's how you get to no. 16: Value! Score 0 to 10 based on your pricing. If you can establish and maintain a value-added premium price versus competition, give yourself credit for being perceived as a value-added brand. It's a judgment call, of course. Sometimes it takes heroic measures just to maintain price parity. WHAT'S YOUR TOTAL SCORE? Have you projected wishful thinking (or natural optimism) onto the numbers? Most people tend to be a bit on the overly optimistic side. Not that the objective total matters. But now put someone else through this same exercise. Would your staff come up with the same numbers? Your distributors? Salespeople? Consumers? Competitors? Where are the most obvious disagreements? Where can you find consensus? Which assets are clearly performing beyond their potential? Which need a little hand holding, or a bandage, or major surgery? Which are a drag on your brand equity? The fact is, every brand asset has to contribute to a value-added brand image to make the machinery work at peak efficiency. But prudent asset deployment calls for putting money, people, time, and energy against the assets with the most leverage. Don't polish the one bright spot if a crucial asset needs repair. Although analysis based on the 16 points is a critical beginning, correction may require help. To get that, it's often an outside professional who can convince management and employees that not only brand assessment but brand action is necessary.3 So check with your current advertising or marketing agency about their experience in brand asset assessment. Don't ask if they have the expertise—nobody ever says, "No, we don't."

CHAPTER TWO

Newspaper and Magazine Advertising

The process of preparing newspaper and magazine advertising described in this chapter serves the same function as a blueprint or detailed drawing in the construction of a garden shed. Using identical plans, the professional builder should construct a somewhat sounder and better looking structure than you—but the shed you produce on your own will be immeasurably improved by following the drawing rather than trying to make things up as you go along. WHY YOU ADVERTISE Preparation and Inspiration When Thomas Edison was asked the secret of his success, he replied, "Two percent inspiration, 98 percent perspiration." You won't have to work nearly that hard. Think of your task as "90 percent preparation, 10 percent inspiration." That preparation starts with a systematic look at why you advertise and what you expect to get out of advertising. Put It in Writing Put into writing your reasons for advertising—all the reasons—and the results you expect the advertising to bring. You need this list to give a sharper focus to the ads you are going to create and, probably even more important, to have a method of evaluating results. Don't expect any one ad to do ten different things or you'll get one-tenth the results . . . or none at all! Set priorities, then focus on the most important. How to Set Goals for Your Advertising In setting goals for your advertising, remember at all times that your results must be quantifiable. Depending on your competitive situation and specific business goals, list the expected results as a definite number or percentage—not "more sales," but, for instance, "5 percent more sales during the week following the ad." If you, like many newcomers to a certain kind of business, have no idea what to expect, put down the number that will justify the cost of the ad if it meets your list of objectives. Regardless of the actual results, whether you like them or not, keep a record in writing.

It is your benchmark for future planning and programs. How to use such a record will be discussed shortly. Typical Advertising Goals Following are some goals a retailer might set. Analogous goals would be set for a manufacturer or a service organization. The sample percentages are arbitrary and are not based on actual case histories. Short-Term Goals • Increase total store traffic by 5 percent during the week following advertising. • Increase the sale of advertised items by 15 percent over the previous week. If you are advertising more than one item, you will want to know how each individual item sold, as well as how all the advertised items sold as a whole. This knowledge gives you information for future promotions, even when sales as a whole do not live up to expectations. Be sure to make a special note of purely seasonal successes, such as pumpkins sold just before Halloween. Make a note of the weather—from great to terrible—plus special occasion successes . . . or failures. A traffic-stopping fire two blocks away can affect business just as much as a hailstorm can. • Increase the sale of nonadvertised merchandise by 5 percent over the previous week. Advertising is usually meant to increase traffic, and that should be reflected in increased sales throughout your establishment. Long-Term Goals • Maintain an increase in store traffic of 2 percent in the month following the advertising, as against the previous year. • Increase customers' satisfaction with products and services. Often it is impractical for a smaller firm to afford professional research on customer or client satisfaction. But informal research is always possible. When customers phone, ask about their satisfaction with your products and service, and whether they are getting the information they want from your advertising and promotions. Make certain you get and read any letters of complaint as well as those of praise. Make sure everyone associated with you knows you are serious about customer satisfaction. Make it your personal priority, and you'll be astonished at the positive results. Where to Get Help in Setting Goals If you are a novice in setting advertising goals, here are some sources of help: 1. Media. The publications in which you advertise, the media, have expert representatives who often have information about advertising campaigns such as yours. Whether you plan a single ad or a yearlong series, speak with these reps about what you might expect from your ads. But remember that their jobs depend on their convincing you of the effectiveness of their publications, so check their sucWHY YOU ADVERTISE 13 cess stories with the people who did the actual advertising—even if they are now your competitors! 2. Your competitors. Take your competitors to lunch—one at a time—and ask them what kind of results they get from their advertising. Chances are, they'll tell you. Almost everyone shows off by talking too much. Analyze your competitors' promotions. Even if they tell you everything you want to know, check. 3. Trade associations. Your trade association probably has an entire library of advertising case histories. Call and ask for this and any other help the association might give. 4. Colleges and universities. Contact the head of the advertising or marketing department (advertising is usually taught as part of marketing and is also located in journalism and communications schools). Explain what you are trying to learn, and ask whether that information is available from either staff or research materials. Expect to pay a consultant fee. (You don't work for free, do you?) The faculty will help if it can. 5. Libraries. Explain your need to the research librarian at your public or professional library. These are extraordinarily knowledgeable professionals with access to networks of information through computer linkups. 6. Build your own research base. If no other information is available, run your ads, set "best guess" goals, and begin to build your own records. You'll quickly have the best database in town and might even be invited to lecture to those whom you previously asked for information. But don't disclose too much. Remember what we said about your competitors. You be the one who does know how to keep your mouth shut, even when you'd much rather show off. Brag about your bank statement, not your ad results.

HOW MUCH TO PAY FOR ADVERTISING How to Budget for Advertising How much you can, will, or must spend on advertising should be decided as objectively as possible; that is, base your decision on reasoning rather than luck or "hoped for" results. To do this, take your advertising goals and calculate, as well as you can, both the "static" percentage-of-sales and the "dynamic" objective way of establishing your overall advertising budget. Both methods are explained below and have devoted followers. After you've become familiar with them, begin by using the one with which you feel most comfortable—but stay with it only as long as it gives you the expected results! A case history. Gaining additional profit by not advertising has been attempted by a number of companies and brands, usually with disastrous results. The nonchocolate milk flavoring, Ovaltine, my childhood favorite, never recovered from such a decision. Not advertising to gain dollars to fight, or profit from a corporate takeover is not an advertising consideration. 1. "Static" percentage-of-sales method. Historically, "percentage of sales" was the way to establish advertising—and most other—budgets. In many businesses it still is. A specific percentage of last year's gross sales, often suggested by industry standards, is allocated for promotional activities. Objectives are proposed but must be modified by the reality of such budgets. Despite the static aspect of percentage-of-sales budgeting, many managers welcome its protection from unrealistic sales projections. Most of them recognize that it "protects" them from realistic projections as well. They simply prefer the relative safety of the known to the projected. 2. "Dynamic" objective method. The objective method is more dynamic and requires a certain daring by management—especially if it's spending its own money. Unlike percentage of sales, which locks in budgets regardless of the current year's goals, the objective method expands promotional budgets to meet what management believes are realizable objectives, regardless of previous years' sales.

Budgeting for Individual Ads Using some of the advertising goals suggested earlier, an individual ad plan might look like . It charts four points to consider in planning: 1. Advertisement goal. 2. Percentage of total ad dollars allocated to your goal. 3. The dollar value for achieving the goal. 4. The time allowed for achieving the goal.

Evaluating Advertising Results In evaluating the success of your ad, as charted in Figure 2.1, the calculation might seem quite simple; however, what if your overall goal is reached but your individual subgoals are not? Does it really make any difference? The answer depends both on the type of establishment you have and the reasons you set your goals. If you are advertising loss leaders to bring new customers to your store, and only regulars show up, you're in a different position from having a sale where your inventory costs have been reduced by a manufacturer, leaving profits the same as at the regular price. These and similar considerations should enter into developing your advertising goals. You want sales, of course, but it requires a different perspective to plan advertising for a funeral home or accounting service than for a hardware store or a farm equipment dealership. In fact, without prohibitively expensive research, how can you get a short-term fix on advertising that aims at long-term results? Fortunately, there is a fairly easy, practical, and inexpensive way to do just that.

Where there is high customer traffic, such as shopping malls, individual stores, banks, and so on, display large-enough-to-read copies of possible future promotions and track the results. These can be fairly simple "nonadvertised specials" or copies of complete possible ads. The preview secret is to give your prospects a benefit for acting now! Your reward is immediate positive, negative, or neutral test results. Two examples show how this works. 1. Ad previewing in a bank. Three possible ads, offering what the bank believes are benefits wanted by its customers, are mounted and placed in the bank's windows and high-traffic lobby. Each ad offers in-person or written information. Each test produces a clear winner, which then becomes part of the bank's advertising campaign. 2. Offer preview. A talk with the sales representative brings a free coffee cup personalized with the prospect's name as Executive of the Year. Hundreds of office managers listen to the sales pitch. Far too few buy for the time spent by the sales force. A different offer is previewed and proves a winning success—both in producing sales and in earning a major advertising award. Getting a Preview of Long-Term Results Although the need you fill may lie months or years in the future, try for some immediate response to your advertising now. If you establish a good relationship before the need arises, you're much more likely to get the call when it does. So do what the movie moguls do before they spend millions on promoting a film: Check it out with a sneak preview. How to Sneak a Preview Purchase or produce a helpful hints flyer along the lines of "10 reasons why you should meet your banker before you need a loan" or "10 things to look for when you're ready to buy a house." The help should be specific rather than general and be directly related to what you do (where to look for dry rot and how to tell it's there rather than "check for dry rot"). The more valuable the advice, the more likely that it will be kept and consulted when a service such as yours is needed. Informational flyers may be available from your trade or professional organization and often are advertised in trade journals. They tend to be inexpensive and may be customized with your name, address, and telephone number at a small additional cost. You can, of course, also produce your own. If several suitable flyers are available, offer a different one free each time you advertise, to see which one gets the best response. Then use that flyer as long as the level of response continues. If your budget is limited to fewer ads than the number of different kinds of flyers available, ask the supplier which one has gotten the most repeat orders. Then use that, providing that it meets your other criteria.

No matter how successful your response, vary the offer occasionally to attract a different audience and to check whether what has been your best draw continues its appeal. Take nothing for granted if you can test to make sure. BUT MICE DON'T BUY MOUSETRAPS: HOW TO FIND THE

AUDIENCE YOU NEED Targeting by Building Profiles Profile building can be critically important for many different kinds of business and the success of their advertising and promotions. If you are a retailer, your customer profile may seem obvious, but there is a simple and inexpensive way to make sure: Ask your customers why they bought what they did at your shop. Since they may not want to tell you, use the same approach suggested for getting help in defining advertising objectives. Ask the marketing department of a nearby college or community college for help in wording the questions and doing the actual interviews. For instance: • Did your customers check advertising before purchasing a product or service and if so, in which medium? • Which publications do they buy and/or get delivered, actually check the ads, read, or just skim? • Which publications do they like best? (This is a check against the "which they read" answers.) • Demographic information, where appropriate, such as age, education, and income, given in approximate ranges. As stressed in the chapter on telemarketing, it is astonishing what people will tell you, when they are asked politely. Often the answers are not at all what you expected and lead to changes in advertising plans. Perhaps equally important, it never hurts to show professional concern for your customers' wants and needs! Manufacturing may require more sophisticated research—and often gives equally surprising results. For example, when a film company produced a series that would explain upcoming surgery to patients, the company "knew" its customer profile. It consisted of family doctors who make the initial diagnoses and surgeons specializing in those fields. But before the filmmaker's advertising agency did anything about creating ads, it did a routine check to corroborate the customer profiles. It took only a very brief telemarketing survey to learn that the true customer—ready and eager to order, immediately, over the phone—was not the doctor. It was the hospitals' senior floor nurses, who were responsible for putting the patients at ease before surgery. The client saved tens of thousands of dollars in two ways: by not advertising to the wrong audience and through earning profits by advertising to the right target audience. Even more important, the company gained insight into the importance of verifying a customer profile—even when you "know" that you know the result before you begin. There's much more about profile building and its use in the chapter on direct mail. So decide to whom you will be advertising before you write a single word. Often, it's not as obvious as it seems. Suppose you have a baby product. Will you advertise to parents, grandparents, pediatricians, toy store owners, supermarket buyers, and so on? Don't work on what to say until you're absolutely clear about two things: 1. The audience you're trying to reach. This may, in fact, be a variety of audiences. The question then becomes one of how many different messages you can get into one ad. Generally, you are better off to concentrate your advertising on one specific target—the "rifle" rather than the "shotgun" approach. To repeat: Don't expect any one ad—or any one medium—to do 10 different things or you'll get one-tenth the results . . . or none at all. 2. What you want your audience to do. Rush to your shop . . . call for an appointment . . . invite you to their office or home . . . send money . . . send for information . . . authorize a trial subscription . . . Vote! Buy! Try! Call! Write! Drive! Fly! Run! Walk! Taste! Imagine! Sleep! And that's just a sampler to get you started. DESIGNING THE AD This chapter will guide you in writing a competent advertisement; however, only God can gift you with the talent to be a designer. Therefore, in the hope that we will be forgiven, we do what real designers do. We borrow. Or as a number of great designers are credited with saying: "The art of creativity is not to reveal one's sources." How to Design Your Ad without Being a "Designer" Look through the publications in which you expect to advertise, and pick out those ads which you feel are well designed and are aimed at your audience. Equally important, they must be the same size as the ad you wish to produce. Try to find several examples, especially those with different amounts of manuscript—what copywriters call "light," "medium," or "heavy." Now pick two or three you like best. These will be your models. Everything you do to create your ad will be based on one of them. The reason for choosing several originals is to give you flexibility in how much you say. But whatever the original has—light copy or heavy, large type or small, with a picture or without— plan to do the same. Avoid the temptation to mix and match—to take design elements from several ads and combine them into a new whole. That is what professional designers often do, but those of us who aren't pros usually botch it up. Eventually, you'll give your manuscript, along with your design model, to a typesetting service and ask them to approximate the original. (You want to avoid lawsuits whenever possible.) Do not do this on your own computer, unless it has a true typesetting program. It won't work! This aspect of advertising is called production and needs a manuscript as well as a design. That's why writing the ad is next. Production, including the wisdom of setting your own ads, follows right after.

WRITING THE AD: THE IMPORTANCE OF BENEFITS The key to writing successful ads lies in training yourself to turn features into benefits—and then to use benefits to sell the product or service. A feature is anything inherent in your product or service, for instance, punctureproof tires on a bicycle, large type in an insurance policy, nonpolluting soap in a laundry. In essence, a feature is what you have put into your product or service. A benefit tells the potential buyers what's in it for them if they use your product or service. For example: • Are your bicycle tires punctureproof because they're made from uncomfortable solid rubber, or is the benefit that these state-of-the-art tires are so safe that riders won't need to carry patching kits and pumps? • Large type in an insurance policy seems an obvious benefit for the elderly, but is it necessary if you're trying to sell to newlyweds? How about "No eye-straining tiny type, but a policy designed to be read and understood!" • Surely you can develop six additional benefits of even greater value to the person you are trying to persuade, no matter what you wish to sell. How to Develop Benefits Even though you want to end up with benefits, begin with features, because they are what you are likely to know best. List each individual feature at the top of a 5 8 index card. Start with what you know, then enlist the help of anyone who has knowledge you may lack or who might catch an item you've overlooked. Once you're satisfied that you've captured all the features, call an old-fashioned brain storming session and explain your problem. You have all these great features, but the people you're trying to sell keep saying, "So what? What's in it for me?" It's the answer to these two questions that are your benefits. THINGS TO REMEMBER IN BRAINSTORMING, WHETHER YOU DO IT BY YOURSELF OR IN A GROUP 1. Use a tape recorder so that you can keep note taking to a minimum. 2. There are no dumb suggestions. 3. Do not discuss individual answers now; that will inhibit the free flow of thought and force participants to defend something they may not quite understand themselves. 4. Bring in a new feature the moment the benefit stream dries up. Keep the action lively. 5. If someone suddenly suggests a benefit for a feature that's already been covered . . . great! 6. Don't let anything negative get in the way of the process. Once you and your features are exhausted, type each one, along with its suggested benefits, into your computer, print them on individual sheets of paper, and distribute copies to the brainstorming participants. Now is the time for critical scrutiny—and for the addition of those benefits that brought you awake in the middle of the night two days after the original session. Ask everyone to criticize, add to, change, edit, or otherwise modify anyone's suggestions and return the lists to you for a final compilation. Whether you'll have another meeting to discuss this final list will be determined by your working situation, but the end result should be a series of features and their benefits, in order of importance for specific audiences. Thus, the same benefit may appear more than once but be given different emphasis, as in details of nutritional value in selling puppy food to veterinarians and careful feeding instructions in selling it to the general public.

Features Instruct, Benefits Sell! Practically no one buys anything solely because of its features—it's the benefits that sell. Thus, you do not say, "the world's best seeds," but "the world's best lawn!" Not "777-horsepower engine," but "from 0 to 135 mph in 3 seconds!" And ask yourself where and how anyone is actually going to want to speed up like that and what other uses there can be for a machine with that much power. You'll continue to discover benefits that will surprise even you—and delight you with their pulling and selling power. Beware of Overkill Make sure that the benefits you claim are actually those the buyer gets. You are legally responsible for any claim made in your promotional materials—for anything that appears in print or on electronic media and for which you may be assumed to have given approval. There are some exceptions, such as an innocent mistake in a price that is corrected immediately at the place of purchase— although not a price designed to mislead! In case of doubt, consult your attorney, or better yet, change the benefit to something else. Advertising is not a game to see what you can get away with; it's one of the few ways of communicating what you hope to sell to potential buyers. The end goal is not to avoid going to jail. It's to make an honest sale from which the buyer will receive genuine benefits and the seller will earn a profit. Developing Your Offer Suppose you've listed every feature you can possibly discover in your product or service and overwhelmed the skeptic's "so what" question about each with a flood of irresistible benefits. Now it's time to consider the offer—the agreement between you and your customers, the promise you make when they buy your product or service. Planning the Offer In planning your offer, three different factors need to be considered: 1. What do you want the reader of the ad to do? For example, go to your store or shop? Telephone for information? Invite you to make an estimate? Send money? 2. What will the customers get if they accept your offer? Offers range from discounts (10 percent off) to service (oil changed while you wait) to promises (service with a smile) to guarantees (unbreakable or your money back). Offers can be implied (Swiss quality) or trumpeted (world's best roofing shingles). They can be limited (offer ends Wednesday) or universal (lifetime guarantee). Whatever the offer, try to match it to the needs and interests of your particular audience. If you're not sure and have no other good way to find out, run two or more versions of the same ad at the same time, changing only the offer, and see what happens. How to do this is covered under advertising production's "A/B Split" a bit later in the chapter. 3. Can you afford it? Can you afford to offer less? Obviously, you will make your offer as inexpensive to you as possible. However, the key is not cost as such, but cost effectiveness or cost per sale. So before deciding on what you can afford, get the best answers possible to four more questions: A. Is this a one-time sale, or are you trying to establish an ongoing customer relationship, and how much is each of these worth? B. How fast must you get your return on the dollars spent for promotion, and will that return come faster if you make the offer more attractive?

C. What do your competitors offer, and should you match that or make your offer even more attractive? What are the likely consequences to them—and you—of an "offer war"? D. What are the immediate costs of these options, what are their break-even points, and what are their payoffs if they succeed? The chances are that you'll have to make an educated guess at some of the answers to these questions. Do it, but keep your guesses on the conservative side. If there are to be surprises, let them be happy ones.

WRITING THE AD: WHERE TO START Every ad is made up of four elements: 1. The headline, commonly called "the head." 2. Body copy, which is everything except the headline and the identifying signature, or "logo." 3. The offer, which is part of the body copy but has to be thought out separately. 4. The logo, or signature, which identifies you and is generally the same as or very similar to your letterhead. My personal way of working is to begin with the offer, go to the body copy, and do the headline last. The offer forces me to understand exactly what I am trying to sell and what the buyer gets in return. Chicken at 49¢ a pound, when the competitors are charging 55¢, requires no explanation; but an HMO or the 27th new restaurant to open this month needs a different kind of enticement. After a rough (preliminary) draft of the offer, I do the body copy. My best headlines have generally grown out of a seed planted in the body, which I suddenly realize would make the perfect head. Of course, once the headline is in place, the entire ad may have to be fine-tuned to fit it, but that won't matter, as long as you work within the ARM framework, which I will tell you about next. Where You Should Start Where you start really makes no difference. Many writers begin with the headline or body copy instead of the offer and work from there. But no matter where you start, the headline is of such crucial importance that we'll treat it in detail first. SUMMARY • Load up with benefits to hit your target. • Plan your offer for your customers' wants, not yours. • When you can't afford the offer, can you afford to offer less? WRITING THE AD: WHERE TO START 23 The Headline (and Illustrations) The headline (and illustrations, if any) are your grabbers. They are the way to catch readers' fleeting attention and get them actually to read what you have to say. To do this, your advertisement, as every other marketing communication, must achieve the three ARM factors.

Think of these as the ARM portion of "I'd give my arm if only they'd buy." So arm yourself with the best headline you can develop to attract attention. Two things your headline must do: 1. Attract the audience that will actually buy the product or at least influence its purchase. Buyers and influencers are not necessarily the end users. Young children neither buy nor influence their parent's purchase of cough syrup, but they are a major factor in deciding on purchases of toys, games, and cereals. Know for whom you write . . . and why! 2. Have carry-over power that will get readers from the headline into the ad itself. Let's assume that you are writing an ad for a bicycle shop that has added a line for senior citizens. In writing your headline, don't try to be clever or funny. That usually fails, even when attempted by professionals. Rather, begin by stating the most obvious fact and let your ad develop from there. For instance, you might try BIKES FOR SENIOR CITIZENS This approach will keep you out of trouble, but is unlikely to attract very many from the audience you want, unless you spice it up with some benefits. Two of the all-time best benefits are "new" and "free," so let's try to get at least one of those into the ad, perhaps as easily as this: NEW! BIKES FOR SENIOR CITIZENS Notice the difference between "NEW BIKES and "NEW! BIKES." In this instance, the second version is probably preferable. With a different product— insurance, for instance—"NEW BENEFITS" might well do better than "NEW! BENEFITS." Always think of what will appeal to your specific audience and write accordingly. But there is still nothing in the headline to get very many readers from "A" to "R"—to motivate Attention into Readership. So let's strengthen the headline with stronger benefits and, if room permits, more of them, like this.

FREE TEST DRIVE OF SENIORS' NEW RECREATIONAL BIKES Free Lessons For Nonbikers Who Purchase Note the change from "SENIOR" to "50-PLUS" in the first headline, and think about how you might make a similar change in the second. In writing headlines, keep refining, with three goals in mind: 1. Broaden the appeal where possible, but take care not to lose your targeted audience. "50-PLUS" may well capture the attention of seniors, plus attract a bonus group in the close-to-senior years. But broaden one step further to "ADULT," and not only have you lost the focus on your real audience, but you've picked up a number of possible meanings of "adult" that will simply confuse your message. In writing your ad, every single word must be considered for the effect it has on the total message, and nowhere is this more true than in the headline. 2. Get at least one major benefit into your headline. "NEW" and "SPECIAL OFFER" show benefits in the first example. The offer might well be the test drive and free lessons spelled out in the second sample, or it might be something entirely different. 3. Fit the headline into the basic design you've elected as your model. Count the number of letters and spaces in the headline rather than its words, and work within that limitation. Don't cheat. A Note on Guarantees, Promises, and Offers If there is to be any limitation or qualification on an offer—such as free lessons only to those who make a purchase—state this immediately in conjunction with the offer. Unless qualified, a "free" offer is legally free to anyone who requests it.

WRITING THE BODY OF THE AD All your hard work in developing benefits will now pay you back, because this part of the ad should just about write itself. 1. Take the benefits you've put on individual cards or sheets of paper, and arrange them in order of importance to the person you are trying to sell. 2. Check your design model, and see how much room you have for copy. 3. Within your space limitation, put as many benefits as will fit, using a small box, • bullet, or check for each. This is the "telegraphic" style and gives a feeling of importance and urgency to your ad: • Lets you write incomplete sentences. • Gets the most benefits in the fewest words.

Features, Too! What does your audience have to know about technical specifications, size, weight, colors, materials, packaging, and so on, to anchor the benefits to reality? Consider "Available in blue only" versus "A rainbow of 14 color selections." Or "1/4-hp motor" versus "3/8-horsepower, three-speed motor with reverse option." Or "All standard sizes" versus "20-gallon drums only." Recall how irritated you get when you respond to an advertisement, only to learn that it left out the one key factor that would have told you it wasn't for you (or when you didn't respond and found out too late that it was for you). Benefits, yes! Pile them on. But don't forget the features. They'll help draw the right customers in and, equally important, keep the wrong audience out.

Identifying Yourself: Your Advertising Signature or Logo Somewhere in every advertisement, the advertiser's logo—the particular way you show your name, address, and telephone number—has to appear. No matter how fancy or plain, be sure that your logo does include your address, phone number, fax, e-mail, and web site, if applicable. Don't assume that the ad is so appealing that your readers will look them up. They won't. Rather, they'll go to your competitors—the ones who make it easy to do business with them. Always remember that no one has to buy from you, so . . . • Make it simple. • Make it easy. • Make it a benefit for the buyer. • Prepare to laugh all the way to the bank.

ONE FINAL CHECK BEFORE TYPESETTING You know the audience you need to reach, and you have developed a cornucopia of benefits and offers that should make them buy. Now is the time to analyze your finished copy and layout for its appeal to that particular audience. Answer the following ARM questions: • Does your headline shout for Attention from your specific audience? • Do your benefits Retain and heighten the interest of that same audience? • Does your offer Motivate the audience to the action you want it to take? If the answers are all "yes," and if the amount of copy matches the model ad you've chosen, you're ready to go to production. PRODUCTION: FROM MANUSCRIPT AND LAYOUT TO FINISHED AD You've picked a design and written the copy. Now all you have to do is set the type and get it to the media in a form acceptable to them. Fortunately, that's the easiest part, and the next few pages will tell you how.

Typesetting Options 1. Outside production service. Turn over the ad to an outside service and let them do everything else. This is the easiest way to go, and not too expensive. 2. Desktop publishing. If you are very skillful at using your computer to set type, try to typeset the ad yourself. But unless the end result looks as good as professional typesetting, turn it over to the pros. 3. Typesetting by your medium. If your advertisement will run in a single magazine or newspaper, find out if the publication offers a typesetting service and at what cost. Often, this is free or low-cost, and many publications take pride in doing a fine job as part of their overall service. Some of these publications will even permit you to run ads they set in other media, so check on that, too. 4. Professional typesetting.

Professional typesetting, which was a thriving industry when our book was first published, has largely disappeared as a standalone enterprise. Designers and design studios have taken this business in-house and the remaining "typesetters" now tend to offer design services also. Typesetting does exist at many quick printing and copy locations, but the majority lack the knowledge of typography that made old-fashioned typesetters such a valuable helper to the do-it-yourselfer. Whether your type is set in-house or outside, here are a few things you should do and know in dealing with typesetters: Things You Should Do • Explain that you are using your sample ad as a model only; it must not be copied so exactly that you might get sued. • Get a cost quotation. Find out if the cost includes any changes and, if not, how changes are charged. Things You Should Know • Typos. Mistakes by the typesetter, called typos, are corrected without any charge to you. • Alterations. Alterations are the changes you make after the manuscript and layout are delivered and the type is set. They are at your expense. There will be a minimum charge for any alteration—even a single comma. • Manuscript. The best way to avoid charges for alterations is to make sure that your manuscript is clean, that is, exactly as you want it. But be prepared to make a few changes even so. Typesetting seldom comes out exactly as we'd like. So make whatever changes you must, but try very hard to make them all at once. That minimum charge comes back each time you request another set of alterations!

Type: Faces, Weight, and Sizes There are thousands of different styles (faces) of type from which to choose, but there is no need to work with more than a very few. To see some obvious differences among them, see Figure 2.3. You may not find the exact same faces on your computer, but they will be close. Major Type Families Every typeface belongs to one of three families: • Cursive type imitates script or handwriting. It has little use in the body of an ad but is sometimes used for headline or logo. • Serifs are the small curlicues or fine lines at the tops and bottoms of letters. This book is set in a serif face. • Sans serif means "without serif" and is any type in that family. The "Major type Families" above is a sans serif face. The Serif Advantage. Most adults find serif type easier to read than sans serif, with a group of serif designs known as "reader faces" easiest of all. Of the tens of thousands of books, magazines, and newspapers published in the United States, practically every one uses such a reader-friendly type. The Sans Serif Advantage. Sans serif, too, has its advantages, chief among them the following: • Compressibility. Sans serif condenses, or compresses, type better than serif does. That is, you can get more letters per inch without distorting the type. • Contrast. Often, it pays to be different. If everyone else is using a serif face, at least consider the alternative. Or you may want to draw particular attention to one portion of your ad, such as a special offer. • Everyone else is doing it. If everyone else advertising to your audience is using sans serif faces, try to find out why. Ask the representatives of the media where the ads run and the advertisers themselves. Better yet, run the same ad both ways and track the results. Unlike designers or authors of books, your interest isn't in typography; it's in sales. Do whatever works! • Reverse type. White or light-colored type on a dark background is easier to read in sans serif than serif (although it is generally harder to read in either typeface than standard black on white, such as what you're reading here). Use reverse type only in headlines, logos, and what ad pros call "violators" (see figure 2.4), those star-bursts, such as the one on the cover, or other shapes that highlight a very bold statement, as in the bicycle ad described earlier. No matter what your designer says never use reverse type for an entire ad, especially in body copy. It slows down the ability to read. • Overprinting. Using sans serif definitely improves the legibility of type printed on top of ("over") a background color or illustration. However, improved does not necessarily make it good. The key is contrast between type and background. Equally important, when seniors are your target, larger type sizes are needed. Always let legibility be your guide. • Subheads. Many designers use sans serif for subheads, with the rest of the ad in serif type. The authors' personal preference for subheads is a bolder (darker) version of the face used in the body of the ad.

When time and budget permit, advertising professionals test the key elements of their ads to learn the best advertising approaches and media. You do the same, and, like them, rely on your business experience and common sense when you can't. When testing is practical, be sure to structure your ads so that you learn what you want to know.1 • Testing two completely different ads for the same product or service is fine, provided that your price and offer are the same for both. Otherwise, how will you know whether the result came from the ad, the price, or the offer? • In testing one key item—a lower or higher price, headline, offer, illustration, and occasionally typeface—leave everything else exactly the same and change the one item being tested only. If, for instance, you change both the price and the headline, how will you know which produced the result you get? If you increased the price and sales increased, too, or even stayed the same, you won't care. But what if sales fall? Was it because of the new price or the new headline? Decide exactly what it is you want to learn, and test that without changing anything else. For example, suppose you wish to test the appeal of the same product to two different audiences. Figure 2.5 shows how this might be done. In each ad, the headline identifies the target audience. In the body of the second ad, the benefit is modified slightly from the first in accordance with the audience's needs. The rest of the copy remains the same. By placing these ads in media that provide cards for reader response, test results were achieved at very low cost. Note how adding a name at the bottom ("call Alice" for one ad, "call Jean" for the other) adds to the ease of tracking results.

Testing: The A/B Split Many newspapers and magazines will run two different ads of the same size in every other copy of an issue, usually at a slight additional charge. This is not one ad in the first half off the press followed by a different ad in the second half. Rather, A/B means that, of the copies delivered to houses, apartments, and offices in the same block, or the copies sold at newsstands, every other one will contain ad A, with the rest having ad B. In publishing terms, that's known as a true A/B split, and it is just about the easiest, most effective, and least expensive way to test the appeal of two different offers, prices, headlines, and so on. Demographic Editions Many publications offer not only A/B splits but also demographic editions. When you purchase a demographic edition of a publication, you purchase a specific location and/or socioeconomic segment of the total circulation. Large-city newspapers offer neighborhood editions that make it affordable for local retailers to advertise in the "big" paper. National magazines offer everything from over 100 test market locations (Reader's Digest) to 1.6 million top businessmen and women (Time). Explore these possibilities with the media representatives, and, if it makes economic sense for you, weigh the factor into your final decision regarding your choice of media for your ad. WHEN TO CHANGE AN AD No advertisement retains its selling power forever. Even successful ads are often improved by testing different headlines, benefits, or offers—or sometimes by such a simple thing as changing and advertising new business hours. But never change a successful ad simply because you've seen it so often that you're sure that readers are tired of it. The chances are they're not. In fact, an even better chance is that they're not aware of it at all and the ad is just starting to do its best work. One of the more counterproductive mistakes made by advertisers is to stop running successful advertising because they are bored with it. They've lived with the ad from conception through all the birth pangs, to its final arrival as a fully developed promotion. They want to move on to something new and are convinced their customers feel the same way. But their customers and prospects probably haven't seen the ad at all, and when they do, they won't pay it nearly the attention the advertiser likes to believe they will. There are only two valid business-related reasons for changing an ad: 1. The ad is no longer cost-effective. 2. A different ad or a different version of the same ad has proven more effective.The Only Excuse for a Failed Ad A second common—and costly—mistake made by advertisers is to invent excuses for advertising that didn't work. Of course, if you are holding a tent sale, and a tornado keeps everyone locked into their cellars, you will certainly take that into account. But if you have a proven offer, product, price, and medium, very little else, except the ad itself, is an acceptable excuse for a failed promotion. Always go back to the three ARM basics of: 1. Attention: Did you get readers' attention, and how might that have been done better? 2. Retention: Did you retain readers' interest through meaningful benefits, and how might these have been enhanced? 3. Motivation: Did your offer motivate the readers to act the way you had expected, and how can you improve the offer? Learning from Success Learning from success is much more pleasant than learning from failure, so don't forget to do that, too. Keep detailed records. Analyze them to discover what you did right, and then apply it in the future. Avoid developing new ads without feedback when feedback is available. Celebrating your successes is much more fun than being creative about excuses.

COOPERATIVE ADVERTISING Cooperative (co-op) advertising is an agreed-on sharing of specified advertising costs or other promotional costs among manufacturers and retailers or analogous groups. Co-op is an arrangement beneficial to both manufacturers and their business partners and an excellent way to expand advertising and promotion dollars. co-op can extend far beyond the traditional print and broadcast media; in fact, many manufacturers now allow Internet advertising under the guidelines of their co-op advertising programs. The list of eligible media continues to grow, varies by manufacturer, and will be reimbursed provided it is agreed on and specified within the manufacturer's plan. What a Promotional Advertising Program Should Specify • Who pays. How much or what percent of the cost of the advertising the retailer and the manufacturer each pay. Written programs should clearly specify he terms and rates for reimbursement.

How co-op accrues. Accruel specifies what goods or services apply to the amount or allowance that is offered by the manufacturer for the advertising, how that amount is determined, and over what period of time. By law, the accrual must be proportional for all like outlets of participants, regardless of size or volume. For instance, manufcturers may not give retailers 5 percent of sales for a 100-unit purchase and 10 percent for a larger volume purchase, thereby unfairly rewarding the larter outlets. The degree of co-op must be the same for every retailer, although it can differ or be absent for wholesalers. Co-op may also be regionalized or otherwise limited as long as it is available to competing users.

Co-op accruals are "use it or lose it" amounts, not an additional discount automatically credited to everyone. Co-op is distributed for specified promotional use and is forfeited unless earned in that way .

• What will be promoted. This need not parallel how co-op is accrued. Often, all of the co-op earned is targeted on one or a few promotional leaders. • When to promote. In planning your co-op advertising, consider any national ad campaigns scheduled by the manufacturer. Agree upon dates, seasons, or tie-in events and keep in mind the cut off date for using the current year's co-op accrual dollars. In specifying dates, consider such possibilities as using unspent Christmas co-op for January sales. • Where and how to promote. National organizations tend to favor name media. However, "shoppers," "penny-savers," and similar media may be a retailer's best buy. Stay flexible. By law, not only must co-op be proportional, it must also be functionally available. That is, it may not be limited to what only the largest accruals can buy. • Message approvals. Both co-op partners are responsible for claims about their products and services. Agree on who creates and who approves the advertising. To prevent conflicts, many manufacturers prepare advertisements and commercials that are easy and inexpensive for retailers to personalize. In fact, a great deal of the advertising that appears in newspapers is manufacturer-created so as to maintain the appropriate product or brand image. • What is not covered. Many co-op programs exclude all creative or preparatory charges and cover only a specified percentage of the net cost of newspaper and magazine space or radio and television on-air time. Be sure to read the fine print of the written co-op plan to see what is eligible for reimbursement. But see Figure 2.6. With the increase in Internet advertising and the use of other alternative media, ACB has expanded verification beyond the traditional print media. Many manufacturers today have modified their co-op programs to allow the use of these media, although they will usually require that the retailer receive prior approval for advertising in selected media. The purpose of a co-op program is to promote the product or service better and sell more of it. If what will work isn't in the current agreement, attempt to add it. Just remember: put it in writing! Auditing Co-Op: How and Why Most companies with substantial co-op programs audit retailer or other local chargebacks through an advertising checking service such as the Advertising Checking bureau (ACB). Local advertisers submit tear sheets of their ads (the actual pages on which the ads appeared) or some other proof of promotional activity, with invoices substantiating the cost. ACB keeps a running total of advertisements that appear in many U.S. newspapers and hundreds of magazines, with their actual cost to the advertiserrs. Like other co-op advertising services, it checks charge-backs and, where necessary, corrects them to their true rate. In most instances, the corrected charge-back is approved by the retailer. When the original charge-backs are too high, an audit report specifies actual rates and an approved co-op amount. In case of conflict, the service, rather than the manufacturer, becomes a party to the disagreement. Thus, rather than a conflict between a supplier and a customer, you get a debate between accountants. If, as can also happen, charges are too low, notifying retailers about this can hardly be surpassed for creating goodwill. Many co-op agreements specify that claims for co op reimbursement will be verified by an auditing service. Such services are in every major and most secondary markets and can be found in the Yellow Pages. Most of them specilize in local and regional media. A few, such as ACB, operate nationwide. If you are the co-op provider, the incremental cost for auditing could prove to be a valuable investment in helping maintain the integrity of your program. In the evolving world of promotional advertising, manufacturers should be certain to remain current in the Federal Accounting Standards board (FASB) regulations concerning advertising documentation requirements and policies.

When changing your telephone number for any reason, several days later call Information as well as your old number to see what happens. And do it every six months even if you don't change. We repeatedly were given a nonoperating number when trying to contact ACB. It was not the first such misinformation in our experience.

NOTES ON THE NEWSPAPER/MAGAZINE ADVERTISING CHECKLIST These notes are a supplement to the material presented in this book (see Figure 2.7). They are not a self-contained substitute for that material. 1. Quotations. The total of all quoted and/or estimated costs accepted from outside suppliers, plus the known or estimated internal out-ofpocket costs. This is the amount given for budget approval in #2. 2. Budget approval. The amount either accepted from #1, or otherwise determined as a fair cost to do the project. If lower than the figure in #1, costs may have to be renegotiated with suppliers or the project modified to fit the dollar allocation. 3. Project approval. Once the project can be done for the amount in #2, a decision on whether the project is worth the cost, no matter how "fair" the individual charges may be. 4. Target audience. Determination of the target audience at whom the ad is focused. Usually this is done as part of a total marketing program. Everything else about this ad must then be controlled by that focus. How else will you decide the message and the media?

5. Message. This tells the writer what is to be said, not how to say it. The actual wording is the job of the writer in #9. 6. Benefits. The benefits keyed to the audience in #4. If none of those benefits seem particularly suited to that group, the choice of those benefits and why that particular audience was targeted must be reconsidered. 7. Headline. The headline's subject, not its wording. Pick the one thing most likely to attract the target audience; usually the key benefit from #6. 8. Offer. Make the offer a major reason to get the advertised product or service from you and to do it now, especially if a competitor's options are available. As the advertiser, do not be afraid to echo your competition. If you can't do better, at least stay even. Note that the offer can appear anywhere in the ad as long as the design gives it such prominence that it can't be missed. 9. Writer. The checklist shows the person who appoints the writer.* If certain things must be said in a specific way, let the writer know before he or she begins . . . and whether this is a legal constraint or a management decision. If the latter, management should be willing to at least consider alternatives.

10. Designer. The person responsible for choosing the designer.* Good designers often surprise, so do not be hasty to say no to what you may not like at first sight. It is the designer's job to know how to appeal visually to the targeted audience. All of us, and especially the younger generation, are becoming more visually oriented. Designers are right more often than they are wrong. 11. Colors. The use of color in newspaper and magazine ads almost always gains readership. So does size. If dollars are set and you must choose one of the two, ask each media representative for facts and figures on which works better in their specific medium. If still undecided,

pick color. For low-cost, striking effects, ask about "spot color," the use of any amount of a single color; just so it does not cover the entire ad. 12. Typesetter. For advertising that requires design skill, use professional typesetting. Limit in-house desktop typesetting to straightforward flyers, reports, and other simple-to-create projects. 13–14. Photography/art. Both who selects the photographer and/or artist and who gives the technical as well as the aesthetic instructions (not necessarily the same person!). Unless the person doing or given the assignment is an expert in art reproduction for newspapers and/or magazines, discuss this with the filmmaker in #16 before any photography or art is ordered (For instance learn about shooting photos for "contrast" or "detail" and what the disk and/or the camera can and cannot "see.") Much more about this is included in the Prepress Checklist. 15. New art. "New art," formerly called "camera ready," is the all-inclusive term for illustrations, photography, and type put into position to create the ad. Once digitized it becomes an electronic file. It is the last chance to change anything at relatively low cost. It includes every instruction to the disk producer or filmmaker in writing. If another department or an outside service or agency does this, the person who assigned the project goes over it with them. For major projects, the disk producer or the filmmaker should be present also. Everyone involved must understand the instructions and understand them the same way. 16. Disk/Film. Preparation of preprinting disk or film also includes proofs (photographic copies of what the printed ad will look like) for final approval, as well as for each publication. The proof is checked against every instruction on the original art to make certain it has been followed. It is literally checked off so nothing is overlooked. Equally important, the proof is examined to see whether those instructions make sense in what is seen now. Newspaper advertisements seldom are as "sharp" (clear) in print as on the proof. If for any reason the ad is hard to read on the proof, it will probably be impossible to read when printed. The original instructions must also specify how many proofs and what kind will be needed. Each medium's rate card has this information. Most ask for one proof; some want more.

17. Shipment. Let the prepress firm ship the film to its destination—even if it is across the street from your office. That is part of their know-how and their responsibility! 18. Media. Does the focus of the media match the target audience focus in #4? If not, why this selection—unless it is the only paper in town? If there is no good medium for what you are advertising, use what is available . . . and work on building a mailing list. 19. Dates. Differentiate

among the four key dates in making magazine selections: A. Closing date. The date by which ad space must be reserved (ordered) for the ad to appear in a specific issue. B. Mechanical date. When the material from which the ad will be printed—usually digitized, sometimes film, or new art—must be at the publication. If art is required, check with the publication to learn exactly what they mean by this term. C. Cover date. The date printed on the publication's cover. D. Out date. The dates on which the magazine will be mailed and when it will appear on newsstands. These may be up to a week apart. 20. Size. Have a reason for the size of the ad. Note that it often costs less overall to create a single larger ad and use it everywhere than to pay for the creation of smaller versions for less important and less expensive media. 21. Space cost. Dramatic discounts are possible when someone advertises fairly frequently in the same medium. Almost all publications combine "space" with "frequency" discounts to make it possible to run more advertising at lower per-ad cost. The media buyer, the person responsible for purchasing the space, should ask media representatives about "rate holders," the smallest ads accepted by a medium, and whether there are any other ways to save. Since media representatives may not be able to negotiate rates other than those given in their rate card, check with the media buying services found in major city Yellow Pages about the possibility of negotiated rates! 22. Notification. Notify or confirm orders, including telephone orders, to each medium by fax or mail. Use a reservation form similar to the one shown in Figure 2.8. Although reservation on a purchase order or letterhead is accepted by practically everyone, the use of a media form gives a better assurance that all pertinent instructions will be covered. 23–29. Mechanical checks. Someone has to be responsible for checking each of these items before anything may be printed. Make sure that the responsible person does check them and signs off in writing. In many organizations, the logo—the organization's name, address, and telephone number—is stored in its own computer file, and must be used from that art. It is an excellent safety measure, providing every such file is corrected when there is a change. Experience shows that practically no one really checks logos. Wise advertising directors make themselves the exception. 30. "As run" copy. Some one person must be responsible for maintaining a file of all ads "as run"; that is, as they actually appeared in each publication. The printed copies should be used for this file. Normally, only a single copy of the page on which the ad appears accompanies the invoice—even when the advertiser requests two or three. So if accounting must see the printed ad before a medium is paid, let them see the original as proof, thank them for their care, and leave with them a reproduced copy "for the record."

CHAPTER THREE

Print Media

WHO READS NEWSPAPERS The simple and truthful answer to "Who reads newspapers?" is "Just about everyone!" Though the trend in newspaper readership is downward, the majority of adult Americans, regardless of income, race, or sex, read either a daily or Sunday newspaper, and many of them read both. Furthermore, they read their paper not only for news and features but according to an Advertising Age study, even more intensely for the paper's advertising, including the classified section. General Audience Newspapers As of September 2001, 1,482 newspapers were published in the United States. Of these, 776 were morning papers, 704 were evening papers,1 and 913 published a Sunday edition. The six-month average circulation of the daily newspapers totaled 55,859,000. Approximately 82 percent of this total, or 45million-plus, is made up of morning papers; the remaining 18 percent, or 9 million-plus, are afternoon editions. Sunday papers, published by 913 papers, totaled 62,020,0002 or over 6 million more than the combined morning and evening daily total. This Sunday total is not as surprising as it might at first appear. Papers sell more copies on Sunday, and the larger-circulation papers are most likely to produce a Sunday edition. (The only papers in the top-100 group not to publish a Sunday edition are The Wall Street Journal and USA Today.) America's largest 100, make up 50 percent of the circulation of all the dailies published. Weekly papers, which are equally important in many smaller communities, add about 8 million for an overall daily/weekly total of 63 million-plus. More than 85 percent of these papers, are delivered to homes, offices, and businesses. The rest are single-copy issues bought from newsstands, retail shops, and vending machines. While the January 2000 circulation of general daily and Sunday papers has shrunk in the past five years, the opposite is true for target audience publications,

Category Publications Paid Free Total Black 125 3,538,000 2,175,000 5,713,000 Community 6,646 20,600,000 28,570,000 29,170,000 Ethnic 167 2,723,000 1,041,000 3,764,000 Gay / lesbian 49 25,000 741,000 766,000 Hispanic 146 1,209,000 5,080,000 6,289,000 Jewish 111 1,259,000 718,000 1,977,000 Military 130 117,000 1,543,000 1,660,000 Parenting 148 156,000 6,499,000 6,655,000 Real estate 91 105,000 2,649,000 2,754,000 Religious 128 4,741,000 338,000 5,079,000 Senior 129 20,743,000 5,045,000 25,788,000 Shoppers 1,413 666,000 60,430,000 61,096,000 Alternative (niche) 128 171,000 7,165,000 7,336,000 Totals 12,641 56,054,000 121,883 178,047,000 Source: Editorial Publisher Publisher International Yearbook 2002.

Newspaper Readership Although industry statistics on readership are best taken with a grain of salt, long experience in this field indicates that the vast majority of delivered general audience papers—75 percent seems a conservative estimate—go to homes or businesses with at least two adult readers. This gives a probable readership of about 110 million adults who have paid not only for news but also to let advertisers try to sell them their products or services!

Advertising tends to take up 40 percent of newspaper space, yet has been and continues to be welcome in practically every home. Have you ever heard of anyone asking to be protected against receiving "junk advertising" in their newspapers—even if it's the same "junk" catalogs and other FSI (free standing inserts) that newspapers write editorials against if it's delivered by mail?

Who Advertises in Newspapers . . . and Why Newspaper advertising is, overwhelmingly, used by local businesses targeted at local sales, though a surprisingly large number of these businesses have no formalized media plan. According to Direct Marketing magazine, advertising in all U.S. newspapers, including supplements, totaled over $49 billion in 2000, a 30% increase over the past five years. Of this amount, the three major categories, in thousands of dollars were:

Records for general advertising have not been subdivided further since 1984. But using percentages based on the ten-year averages kept from 1974 to 1983, the totals would be: Retail Dept. Store General Auto Finance Classified 51% 6.5% 6.9% 0.025% 0.035% 35% These totals includes national advertisers, such as automotive, soft drinks, alcoholic beverages, clothing, and cosmetics. Those firms are willing to pay a higher "national" rate for three reasons: 1. To increase sales of their products in local outlets. 2. To show local retailers that they are supported by national headquarters. (A campaign I directed aimed at retailers selling the Rand McNally Road Atlas used posters on the sidewalk side of buses where retailers were most likely to see them even while inside their stores.) 3. To make certain that the national advertising message is given exactly as the corporation wants it presented. WHO READS MAGAZINES If we consider only those magazines that carry advertising, according to Media Research more than 90 percent of all American adults read at least one magazine per month, with the average adult reading two magazines per week and spending about one hour with each. Magazine Categories SRDS, a huge database to be discussed shortly, divides magazines into four broad categories: 1. Consumer 2. Agrimedia 3. Business to Business 4. Professional Scholarly publications, a category that would add thousands of additional titles to the list, are so specialized and often of such small circulation that only those wanting to advertise to those fields concern themselves with their rates. Unlike "scholarly" magazines, "educational" media are in the business category aimed at the preschool through university market. HOW TO PICK PRINT MEDIA FOR ADVERTISING The easiest way to pick media is by how well they reach your target audience(s) (TA)—the audience you want to reach. To do this, check on where other advertisers trying to reach the same targeted audience are advertising in a consistent fashion. But don't just look. Do as you did when new to setting objectives. Telephone advertisers. Explain that you are a novice and ask for anything they might tell you about the success of their ads in specific publications. Next, call advertisers who use a medium only once or a few times and ask the same questions. Ask, too, which media they would recommend that might be more effective. People love to give advice, so be sure to check whether or not they actually do advertise in the places they recommend.

WARNING! BEWARE OF "THE RULE OF TWO" An often quoted "Rule of Two" states: "See an ad once, it's a test; see it twice, it's a success." Do not take this at face value in trying to evaluate where, what, how often, and, most important, why others advertise! Rather, see the "Rule of Three," which follows shortly.

Before using the Rule of Two—or any other rule like it—to evaluate a competitor's advertising schedule, consider the following three points: 1. Response request. Is there any response requested in the ad? If the reader is not urged, or at least asked, to do something, as in Figure 3.2, how can you know the ad's results? • "1/3-OFF" qualifies as a hint. • "BRING THIS

COUPON TO GET 1/3-OFF TILL WEDNESDAY!" qualifies as a test. 2. How to quantify. Is there an obvious or subtle way to quantify; that is, to know responses to the ad? For instance, is there a coupon or reply card that is coded to each medium and issue, or a telephone extension or name for which to ask? (See Figure 3.2.) 3. Time to quantify. Before assuming that good results are why the same ad was repeated, check to see whether there was enough time between issues to permit evaluation of results before the next ad was run. In a daily newspaper, that can be as little as three days. In weekly publications, rescheduling an ad even a single day after it appears can mean one to five weeks before it will run again. In most monthly magazines, the wait will be two to four months.

Seeing the same ad over and over doesn't prove anything about its results. The Rule of Two is based on the action of direct marketers for whom "advertising" and "sales" are one and the same. Do not expect it to be the reason for most other advertisers' scheduling!

"The Rule of Three" The advertising "Rule of Three" states: "An ad must appear at least three times in media read by the same audience before you can expect it to be seen (paid attention to) once." This does not mean before anyone will see it once, but before it will be noticed at least once by the majority of your target market audience. In print media, national advertisers consider a range of 3 to 10 exposures as the minimum required for effectiveness.

The Rule of Three (or "Three Hit Theory") has primary value for longerterm "institutional" advertising targeted at brand recognition rather than the immediate response wanted by many retailers. Note that successful retailers and retail chains—from groceries to computers to autos—often do both kinds of ads. IF YOU DON'T KNOW WHERE TO ADVERTISE For anyone, beginner or longtime media professional, the guides to the full range of options on advertising to a specific audience or in a particular field are the SRDS services. The print editions are in many public libraries and practically all professional advertising media departments, which also have access to the online versions. These huge databases, available online and in paperbound volumes, are frequently updated. They give detailed information, field by field, on practically

every medium that accepts advertising. Individual SRDS guide titles,4 as this is written, include the following: • Consumer Magazine Advertising Source™ • Business Publication Advertising Source® Includes Card Decks,5 Health Care • SRDS Media Planning System™ A new online media planning solution. Permits seamless budget, schedule, and campaign management, using SRDS consumer and Business data. • Newspaper Advertising Source® • Community Publication Advertising Source™ • Circulation In-depth analysis of newspaper circulation • TV & Cable Source® • Radio Advertising Source™ • Direct Marketing List Source® • Interactive Advertising Source™ Web sites that accept advertising • Out-of-Home Advertising Source™ Twenty-one away-from-home or office media such as billboards, transit, in-flight, and so on • The Lifestyle Market Analyst® • SRDS International Media Guides™ • Technology Media Sources™ • Hispanic Media & Market Source™ An additional SRDS service covers the mechanical aspects of production, that is, how to get each kind of ad physically ready for a specific medium. But you are unlikely to need that unless you are responsible for furnishing the materials for the ads to many advertising media. The same information is available on an individual basis from any of the media you decide to use.

they go through a series of uniformly numbered segments of specific interest to advertisers. Thus, categories 4–7 always explain basic costs, and category 10 covers the availability of premium positions for advertising, such as the page opposite the table of contents. Many advertisers believe that these locations get exceptionally high readership and are willing to pay a premium to have one of their ads appear there. If premium positions are not listed—or present on a rate card—they may be available by request on a "first-come" basis. (One of my greatest advertising coups was to get ads for a single client on all covers of all programs of their industry's most important trade show by asking and paying for the space 18 months in advance of publication. No one had ever asked before—and a special meeting of furious, and much larger, competitors foreclosed the same option for anyone, including themselves, in the future.)

Reliability of SRDS Data SRDS does not itself research its information but uses data provided by each publication on an issue-by-issue basis. Many of the publishers supply information on circulation in a standard format that is audited by the Advertising Bureau of Circulation (ABC), an agency very much like a CPA firm. Whether or not the information is audited is not necessarily an indication of its reliability. The auditing process is quite expensive and unaffordable by some new publications and publications with a small circulation. Other publications have a long history of satisfied advertisers and feel no need to go through auditing. Auditing is, however, a factor you should consider, especially with publications that have multiple audiences, not all of which are your potential customers.

Before you decide on any of them, however, ask each publication why you should use it to reach your specific audience, and then make your evaluation as you would any other investment—including the possibility that you should switch your promotional effort to direct mail or some other medium. Don't fall into the trap of advertising just to see your name in print.

HOW TO RESEARCH A SUBJECT Though even the SRDS services can't cover every subject, try them first. For online directories, flexible search optons are available. You can search by classification groupings, individual titles, and keyword. You can also narrow your search to just media that are audited. If you still can't find what you need, phone the SRDS Listing Locator Service at (800) 851-7737 or visit them online at www.SRDS.com. If, as is likely, you do find your category, you can link directly to additional planning information, such as audit statements, online media kits, and media web sites. You can also communicate directly with the right media personnel using e-mail hotlinks within a listing. For printed directories, check the classification groupings near the front. If your subject is not there, turn to the index of individual titles and look for a keyword. Ask a few of your larger competitors, too. They want to keep their trade media in existence by finding additional advertisers. It is possible that no specific medium exists for your product or service. In that case, consider a more general publication that's likely to be read by your audience (the Sunday edition of the New York Times by college presidents, for instance, or The Wall Street Journal by wealthy retirees), providing your reaching them that way has at least the potential of being profitable. If, as is likely, you do find your category, contact the appropriate media and ask for a Media Kit information package. Request several copies of each publication to get an idea of its editorial content as a "home" for your message. Each medium's representative will probably also wish to meet with you. You can arrange that at your convenience.

CHAPTER FOUR

Flyers, Brochures, Bulletins, and Invitations

FLYERS AND BROCHURES: HOW THEY DIFFER In standard trade usage, a flyer is made from a single sheet of paper. Figure 4.1 shows just eight of the different formats that a flyer may assume. By contrast, a brochure is in booklet format. In working with outside sources, find out what distinction they make, so that you both speak the same language. Because different suppliers may have different definitions, keep your internal nomenclature consistent and "translate" as you go along. A BRIEF MANUAL OF PROCEDURES Procedures for creating flyers and brochures should be the same whether you do everything yourself, are part of an internal team, or supervise outside resources. The procedures apply to everything from simple do-it-yourself projects to the most sophisticated agency-produced materials. As with every promotion, creating a flyer or brochure is a five-step process: 1. Learn, or decide on, the purpose of your promotion. 2. Establish a time frame and remain within it. 3. Establish and remain within a budget. 4. Write and create the promotion. 5. Produce and distribute the promotion. This is covered as part of Chapter 6 "Direct Mail," and in greatest detail in Chapter 16. Let's consider each of these points in more detail. DECIDING ON A PURPOSE The "Target" Audience Begin by determining to whom the piece will be addressed. The type and amount of information you include should be guided by its use. For instance, senior management will require a preponderance of financial data, the engineering depart .

Always put more detail—whether hard data or a sales pitch—into your printed promotion than into your sales call. There is no way your readers can question your flyer or brochure, so give them everything they need to make them decide your way.

An extensive guide to what and how much to write begins in a few pages. But don't jump there yet. Though writing comes first, there's a lot more to do before the actual writing begins. Using the Promotion Knowing how and by whom the piece you produce will be used is critical to its creation. Will it contain "high" or "low" information; that is, must it generate a sale or produce a lead? Will it be mailed? Placed on the Internet? Distributed by a sales staff? Included in packages? Posted on bulletin boards? Used at trade shows? Or all of these? Let's consider each of these options in turn. Mailing Mailings can be self-mailers; that is, mailed without envelopes or mailed inside of envelopes or other containers. They may go by first class or several variations of "Standard" bulk shipping. You may include a coupon or a reply form or request the recipient to write, call, or fax. These and other mailing options and decisions require a chapter all by themselves and are covered in Chapter 6. Use by the Sales Staff Your promotion can be a visual aid during a sales call, a leave-behind reminder, or both. It can be "Let me walk you through this flyer, which illustrates the important points about our service," or "Let me just leave you this brochure, which highlights the points we've been talking about. You can look it over with engineering, and I'll call you about an order on Tuesday."

Some "political" points must also be considered. For example, in larger organizations, how will the sales staff react if the only address shown on flyers and brochures is the home office? Conversely, how will the home office react if all the responses go to the field? As the advertising or promotion director, you may be the only person involved in the promotion who works for "the company," so resolve any such conflicts before your creative efforts begin. Enclosures Make sure that your promotion piece fits into the package. Is your piece the first thing you want seen or the last, and how can you be certain that it will be seen at all? Join the packaging design team first and the packaging crew later. There's no substitute for hands-on experience in this phase of promotional activities. Distribution at Trade Shows If you use "help yourself" literature bins at conventions, meetings, or other events, how much of the promotion piece do the bins show: the complete page, the top half, or the top few inches only? The answer will affect the design of the piece, so do let the designer know. Internet Use Thanks to digitized production, practically any flyer or brochure can be placed on the Internet. They can also easily be modified for the specific medium or any other medium. Think multimedia from the beginning! ESTABLISHING A TIME FRAME AND TIME LINES A time frame is the time allowed for the complete project. A time line details the time for each of its subprojects, such as researching, writing, designing, editing copy, typesetting, and doing artwork. For any project involving outside resources, your time frame and budget are totally interrelated. Costs are affected by time allocations, and completion dates may not be flexible. The brochure that says "Visit our booth for a special discount" will do you no good whatsoever after the exhibit closes—no matter how creative the excuses are for not getting it done. Individual time lines are established by working backward from a targeted end date and allocating completion dates and responsibility for each of the following benchmarks: • End date. When the project must be completed and what "completed" means: printed, distributed (how?), or received (by whom?). • Distribution. The dates for each aspect of distribution, including mailings and warehousing of extra stock. • Printing and bindery work. The time from the completion of printing film or disk to the delivery by the printer of usable printed pieces. For flyers and brochures, a separte bindery may be involved in collating or folding, or the printers may do this themselves. The time line schedules them both. • Copy, design, and layout. Who will do copy, design, and layout and who must approve them are often the most flexible elements of the time line, especially if they are done by internal staff. What is sometimes forgotten is that they are also the foundation on which everything else is built. Constructing that foundation is discussed in detail almost immediately in the upcoming section "Creating the Promotion." • Final disk or art, prepress, and proofing. These subjects are covered in detail in Chapter 16. Check there; schedule here. ESTABLISHING A BUDGET There are two types of budgets, and they must not be confused. Both are fixed, but they are based on different conditions: 1. Administrative budget. A specific amount is allocated, and costs must not exceed that amount. 2. Estimate-based budget. Costs are estimated, and projects are then approved, rejected, or changed based on the estimates. The budget becomes a time line consideration when it must be approved by someone other than yourself before any work may start. If this is mandated, build in time for getting estimates and quotations, as well as the approval itself. CREATING THE PROMOTION: AN OUTLINE The outline that follows is written as if you were the promotional supervisor of a large organization. Exactly the same procedures apply to the one-person shop or any size of organization in between. 1. Purpose. The purpose of the piece is the most important reason or reasons for preparing it; for instance: (a) to use ("walk through") during sales calls, (b) to distribute at conventions, and (c) to mail for leads and/or sales. Make an absolute limit of three. (How many can be "most" important?) Put them in writing! 2. Sources. Determine who will provide the information needed to write and design the promotion and when they will be available. Get a backup source, if possible. 3. Check and approve. Establish responsibility for the accuracy of information about the product, legal clearance, editorial clearance (spelling, grammar, the house style), and sales input. Determine who will edit—rather than write—review, and have final approval of the project. Only one person can have final approval!

4. Concepts and presentations. Depending on how you and your organization work, you may go through a series of concept presentations or go directly to final copy and layout. In either case, the materials must be put through the following steps, whether they be taken mentally while talking to yourself or in formal presentations to others: A. Organization. Organize all your information in the order of importance to the specific audience that will see the printed piece. After it is organized, you can decide how much of the information will actually be used and the style in which it is to be presented. B. Emphasis. Decide which points are to be stressed and which is the most important point of all. Make the latter into your headline. C. Illustrations. Decide on photographs and other illustrations: how many there will be, what kind they should be, and where to get them. D. Response. Determine what you want the reader to do and give them a reason to do it. This is the most frequently understated element in promotional literature. As advertisers, we tell the recipient everything, except why we want them to read the material. E. Policing. Policing is neither proofreading nor editing, but a final check against #1, your stated purpose in producing the promotional piece. That's why we put that purpose into writing. It's very easy to get so carried away with our creativity, that we forget what we set out to do. Once the basic concept has been developed, preliminary or "draft" copy and possible designs are produced. In organizations with several layers of management, these are the versions presented for managerial comments or approval. Note that detailed revisions may be required for draft copy and designs, as some managers can't visualize promotional materials until they see them in quite finished form. During my years as an advertising account executive, I'd reminded my clients—as gently as I knew how—that they were paying for all the changes they order. As employees reporting to management, you must—equally gently—give

notice of impending deadlines.

A BASIC DESIGN CONCEPT The One-Third Guide For a one- or two-page piece (each page is one side of a sheet of paper, not the sheet itself), allow approximately one-third of the space for each of the following • One-third for headlines and subheads, plus information about ordering or a coupon and your logo—that is, the special way you identify yourself. Frequently, your logo is also the way your name, address, phone, fax, e-mail, and website appear on your letterhead. • One-third for illustrations, including charts, and captions. • One-third for general copy; that is, the "body" of the ad. For three pages or more, use the two-page guide for the first page and the last page, and then divide the remaining space so that you use half for copy and half for illustrations. Of course, these are suggested guidelines only, but they will give you a balanced approach to an inviting presentation.

Tell your readers how to order or to get whatever you have to provide. If there are options, explain them. Make it easy. This is not an IQ test for your customers. Make the information complete. Restate the offer, its benefits, and its price. Include toll-free phone, fax, and e-mail, if available. Give the address to write to. List a specific department for information if there is one. Include anything that will expedite a response.1 • Picture captions. Copy for picture captions must be orchestrated just as carefully as that for any other element. The illustrations are there to help get across the overall message. Like your subheads, pictures and their captions should tell your basic story all by themselves.

With the guidance offered here, you can produce your own manuscript ("copy"). But few of us are given the skill to create our own professional-quality design or layout— that is, the overall visual impression and detailed specifications that make a flyer or brochure work. Unlike newspaper and magazine advertising, for which you can find an existing model to follow, printed pieces tend to be too individualistic for that approach. So use a design studio if you can afford it. If not, you have several other options. All but one are quite inexpensive. However, the somewhat more costly one will also be the easiest for you and give you more time for other things.

Tell the studios or freelancers what your project is, what your time frame is, and, if possible, your budget for design and final art. If you have no way of estimating design costs, interview a few of the designers first, and then arrive at a figure based on their quotations. Make sure to schedule the interviews. Tell the candidates they will have 1 hour: 20 minutes to present samples with their charges for everything they show; 20 minutes for you to present your project; and 20 minutes for them to ask any questions. An hour should be adequate with the likely candidates. For simpler projects, allow one week for quotations. For more complicated promotions, allow two weeks. Cost Factors in Working with Outside Designers Whether you work with a freelance designer, a design studio, or an advertising agency, the following factors will affect your costs: 1. Time available to complete the project. Begin by asking potential suppliers their normal time needs for a project such as yours. What you consider a rush project may be their regular schedule. 2. Quality of manuscript. Has your copy been given final approval, or will there be repeated copy changes that will require new layouts? Because you pay for each new version, find out how they are charged. 3. Number of versions required. Many clients want to see two or three (or more) designs from which to choose. For major projects, this is a recommended procedure, but get costs quoted in advance. For routine flyers or brochures, get a single design. It will be the one the designer considered the best of the several he or she attempted before deciding on the one you are shown. 4. Degree of layout "finish." This refers to how polished the layout must be. There are three generally accepted variations: "rough," "semicomprehensive," and "comprehensive." What these three terms mean varies with everyone who uses them. Have prospective designers show samples of each kind of finish and explain the difference in their costs. With most commercial art now prepared on a computer, the differences may be minimal. 5. Preparation of disk or new2 art. Most designers prefer to do the new art. Let them do it. Not only will you get a better end product, but you will have a happier designer, eager to work with you again in the future.

1. Quotations. The total of all quoted and/or estimated costs accepted from outside suppliers, plus the known or estimated internal out-ofpocket costs. This is the amount given for budget approval in #2. 2. Budget approval. The amount either accepted from #1, or otherwise determined as a fair cost to do the project. If lower than the figure in #1, costs may have to be renegotiated with suppliers or the project modified to fit the dollar allocation. 3. Project approval. Once the project can be done for the amount in #2, a decision on whether the project is worth the cost, no matter how "fair" the individual charges may be. 4. Target audience. Are you trying to force different audiences' needs and interests into a single piece? You'll probably lose more in sales than you gain in promotional

savings. Do this only if you have no way to reach each group individually. 5. Purpose. How the item advertised will be used and which use—if there are several—is the most important. Every other item on the checklist must keep the purpose in mind. 6. Overall focus. What the message is to achieve as a whole. The general "feel" of the complete piece. 7. Headline focus. Based on the benefits keyed to the target audience in #4, the one thing you hope will make the reader stop long enough to learn more about your message. Not the words—leave that to the writer in #10—but the thought! 8. Subhead focus. Sell here if you can. But more important, get across the focus message from #6, even if the subheads are all that is read. If #7 and #8 are a 10-second outline that tells your story, you probably have a winner! 9. Response. What you hope the reader will do after reading the piece. If the answer is "nothing special," why are you producing the flyer or brochure? Make the offer a major reason to get the advertised product or service from you and to do it now, especially if a competitor's options are available. 10. Writer. The checklist shows the person who appoints the writer. If certain things must be said in a specific way, let the writer know before he or she begins . . . and whether this is a legal constraint or a management decision. If the latter, management should be willing to at least consider alternatives. Specify whether you want "roughs" or a best effort "finished copy" as first draft. Better yet, ask the writer to produce finished copy, but treat it as a draft. But make sure that you let the writer know you are doing this. Writers tend to get hysterical if it comes as a surprise, after they're done. 11. Designers. Will copy be written to fit the design, or will the design be based on the copy? If different persons do #10 and #11, make sure that they can work as a team. Good designers often surprise, so do not be hasty to say no to what you may not like at first sight. It is the designers' job to know how to appeal visually to the targeted audience. They are right more often than they are wrong. 12. Typesetter. For reasonably simple styling, turn to desktop equipment and set your own type. Give your designer samples of your in-house type faces, so the copy can be marked to match. For pieces that require design skill, use professional typesetting, now most often supplied by your designers. Be sure they understand the importance of type legibility! (See Figure 2.4) Too often designers sacrifice "sell" for "award." All other factors being equal, nothing heightens the appeal of your product or service like skillful professional typography! 13–14. Photos/ Art. Determine who selects, orders, and supervises photography and art. In addition to know-how, it will probably take time. Unless the person doing or given the assignment is an expert not only in art but also in reproduction for commercial printing, this should be discussed with the prepress firm in #16 before any photography or art is ordered. Much more about this in the Prepress Checklist in Chapter 16. 15. Final disk or "new" art. With desktop publishing, you'll probably create simpler art and type on your computer. If you are new to desktop, find out how to make your work practical for use by your prepress firm. For outside production, this is the last chance to change anything at relatively low cost. Put every instruction to the prepress firm in writing. If another department or an outside service or agency does this the person.

who assigned the project goes over it with them. The prepress firm should be present also. Everyone involved must understand the instructions and understand them the same way. 16. Prepress OK. You approve the film by checking its proof. Check everything against the instructions on the hard copy, and check the job as a whole. Better yet, if you work in an organization with film and printing specialists, turn to them for help. It's their job. Let them do it. For newer filmless printing, see Chapter 16. 17. On-press OK. Go to the printer for on-press approval. If not, printers will "hold the presses" for approval and take the material being printed to you—at hundreds or thousands of dollars for press and staff waiting time. But what will you do if you want more on-press changes? Wait in your office again . . . and again. You go to the printer! 18. Page size. Take the original layout to the printer as soon as it is done. Ask your printer if a small decrease or increase in the page size can make a large difference in savings. If the printer says yes, and the new size is practical, tell the designers. It's easier for everyone if they create the design with the new size in mind. 19. Number of pages. For ease of folding, the most economical number of pages usually is a multiple of four (4, 8, 12, and so on). Does deciding on the number of pages precede the creative effort or follow it? Why? 20. Color(s). Selecting colors is subjective, but it's also an art. Accordingly, have it done by an artist if possible. Just make sure that the color choices work for sales as well as aesthetics. Not too many of us can read white type inside a light blue background or light blue printed on white. 21. Paper stock. Where only a specific stock will do, use it. Where options are possible, check your printer or paper merchant for what they have on hand. For some projects, the use of two different papers may bring dramatic savings. Ask! 22. Film preparation. If someone other than your printer prepares the film, be sure that the filmmaker knows that printer's needs. Make certain that they speak with each other, not only through you. 23. Printer. Different printers have different capabilities based on equipment, experience, and expertise. Selection of a printer and prepress firm is best done by an in-house specialist, if one is available. If not, become one by asking your associates in other organizations. Visit their suppliers with them if possible. That's how we learned most of what we know . . . and that's how we continue to learn. 24. Distribution. Determine what "distribution" means: How many flyers or brochures will be used for mailing, shipping to staff, warehousing, and so on? Requests and orders for your pieces may come from anywhere. But for request approval and filling of orders, a single person must be in charge. 25–30. Mechanical checks. Someone has been assigned to check each of these items before anything may be printed. Make sure that they do check them and sign off in writing. In many organizations, the logo, address, and phone numbers are preprint or in an approved computer file, in a variety of styles and sizes, and must be used from that art, an excellent safety measure, provided that every such logo is dated and thrown out when there is a change. Experience has shown that practically no one really reads logos. Make yourself the exception. 31. Printed samples. Printed samples generally get wide distribution. Set up a system that won't force you to reinvent the distribution list with every piece produced. As with newspaper and magazine ads, every piece must be coded and a permanent file maintained. I astonished a client by still having a mailing the client wanted to recreate and that the agency had done 15 years before. BULLETINS, INVITATIONS, AND INVITATIONAL BULLETINS Bulletins and invitations are widely—and successfully—used for business-tobusiness seminars to sell products and services. They are discussed together because, for advertising and promotional purposes, their uses are frequently the same. Bulletins are also used for two other purposes with which you may be involved as a creative resource: 1. Bulletins that must be posted, but that no one reads. State and federal offices, personnel and accounting departments, and senior management (among others) issue materials that must be placed on bulletin boards. However, unless the information displayed has real and immediate application to the audience for whom it was written, it is simply ignored. If you ask how that audience knows it can, with impunity, ignore such bulletins, the answer is, they just do. 2. Bulletins that must be posted and that everyone reads. Often issued by the same sources as in item 1, they give information on newly issued or revised mechanical, safety, or material-handling instructions, on public or private requests for assistance, and many other things. The list is endless. In this case, the audience knows what it must not ignore. The preceding two categories, insofar as they require promotional expertise, can be considered flyers and handled as such. Most often, there are models that can be followed and desktop publishing that can be used to produce the disk or new art. The Challenge of Optional Posting A third category of bulletins is of much more concern to advertising and promotion than the foregoing two. This is the bulletin that no one is required to post, although everyone who sees it should want to . . . and want to read it, too! Usually distributed by mail, it has to jump the initial hurdle of the mail room or secretarial censor, pass its second barrier of managerial scrutiny, and, most difficult of all, crash through the stone wall of passerby indifference. Because your bulletin competes for posting with all the others received at its destination, the challenge is formidable. Your likelihood of success is directly related to a slight modification of the first insight given in this book, which said, Keep it simple . . . keep it specific . . . and you're likely to keep solvent. Apropos of bulletins, the insight would urge.

Who Decides What's Posted? Even if you're sure you know who controls the posting of bulletins at the places to which you mail them, call a dozen of these places at random and ask to speak with the person in charge of putting up bulletins. If the operator does not know, ask for personnel. People will tell you almost anything if asked politely, so remember what you want to learn: • What happens when a bulletin is addressed to an individual by name? • What happens when a bulletin is addressed to a title (say, vice president of finance) or a job description (e.g., person in charge of posting financial training bulletins)? • Does the size of the bulletin make any difference to its being posted? Which sizes are actually used? • Does how the bulletin is received (e.g., in an envelope, as a self-mailer, hand delivered) make any difference? • About what percentage of bulletins received actually get posted? • Why?

The steps in the posting process will tell you how to address and how to send your mailing, as well as what message, if any, to put alongside the address. Usually, a purely informative message, such as that shown in is adequate. The combination of the right name or title, together with an appropriate "teaser"—that is, an interest-focusing outside message—will likely get your bulletin posted. Now all you have to do is to get it read and acted on.

How to Get Your Bulletin Read For posting on a bulletin board, get all the excitement and information on a single page. Don't force your audience to see the other side to understand your message. You are producing a kind of billboard, not a brochure!

"additional training" that is of interest to employers may translate into better pay, job security, a quick chance for advancement, or all three for employees. Just don't be too clever or cute. Save that for the section on invitations, which is discussed next. • Present the benefit in the largest, boldest, easiest-to-see type. You want to capture the attention of the casual passerby. So make it easy to read from a reasonable distance. • Label everything. Mention the time, date, place, cost, anything free, what to bring, what the reader will get to take home, how to participate, and so on. • Sketch a simple map. Do this for locations away from the home, the neighborhood, or work. Give distances from known locations (e.g., "approx. 3.2 miles west of Exit 89 on State Highway 17"). • Add a "Take One" as a reminder. Include the map. Your printer will know a variety of ways to do this. • Give a destination phone number. Do this for people like me, who get lost going around the block. Make the information complete, but keep it as simple as possible. Bulletins often are read in passing. Make it possible to do just that. As a safety factor, place a small "Please post" request in one corner. Always tell people what you'd like them to do. Don't make them guess. Bulletins for Fun Events Fun events, from puppy beauty contests to the Fourth of July picnic and the Santa Claus parade, may seem exceptions to the rules for getting your bulletin posted on a bulletin board. They're not! It's the event that's the fun. The bulletin must still give every bit of information needed to make the event happen. It's certainly all right to lighten the mood, provided that you don't lose the message.

INVITATIONS All of us have received invitations to events that made us a captive audience for a sales pitch—from the chance to meet the candidate to hearing an ex-President try to sell time-sharing condominiums. Whether it's Tupperware in your living room or executive jets at the Paris Air Show, the party proves an effective sales tool, and the one thing every party has in common is an invitation. This section focuses on inviting people together for business reasons— specifically, to inform them, persuade them, or sell them—and perhaps all three. It is not concerned with purely social or personal functions, although the suggested method of structuring an invitation is practical for both. How to set up the function itself is covered in the chapter on conventions, beginning on page 272. A Magical Word Invitation is one of those magical words, like free, new, and now, that many prospective and current customers accept uncritically. You are "invited" in magazine and newspaper ads, by radio and television commercials, on bulletin boards, on the Internet, by fax, and in the mail. All of these take advantage of the built-in association of "invitation" and "enjoyment." It is this expectation of a pleasant experience that makes invitations such an effective sales tool and one that should be more widely used. Invitations even let you bring together fierce competitors who have nothing but you in common. Think of fitting new golf shoes to shoe retailers at a golf outing, perhaps as a surprise before teeing off. Or what about a winetasting session for wine merchants as they sail along on a moonlight cruise. A bit of imaginative soft sell can do wonders. A Word about Design Invitations permit even the least creative among us to become designers. When the event itself has a festive feel, almost anything you develop in typography and layout should work, provided that you include the eight pieces of information from the model that follows. For a more formal feel, look through any stationery store, card shop, or "quick" printer's sample book and pick a model invitation to follow.

Structuring Your Invitation The basic invitation has an eight-part structure that adapts to almost any occasion. Although you may not want to use all eight parts, at least consider each one to make sure that it can be skipped. To show how this works, let's produce an invitation to attend a demonstration of a solar-powered car (see Figure 4.5). 1. You are invited. Invitations imply an enjoyable event. The very word "invitation" prepares the recipient to be well disposed toward what comes next, so make that word prominent and the very first thing that's seen. 2. To the first public presentation. Generally the single most important part of the invitation. Use your utmost inventiveness to make attending the event a benefit. Translate attendance into what the attendees will carry away, and then state that as a promise. For instance: • The most exciting test drive of your life • Your chance to get frank answers from . . . about . . . • A full month of free . . . • Machine tools you will never have to sharpen • Get richer! Get smarter! Get ahead! 3. Of a truly functional. Make the description of the event too valuable or appealing to ignore. If a large part of that appeal lies in a guest of honor or a presenter, let your invitation explain who the person is—even if everyone should know who he or she is. (For presentations, always use the best presenter rather than the person most knowledgeable on the subject if the two are different. But always have the latter there to help answer questions.)

4. Saturday, June 24, 10 A.M. Before setting a date and time, make certain that no conflicting activity will keep your most important guests away. Call and ask, then "confirm" later as a reminder just before the meeting date. 5. Zip-Along Racetrack. Make the location a benefit if possible. Glamorize it (e.g., historic, beautiful, unique), and make it a place that is easy to get to. As with bulletins, provide a map for people who drive and a telephone number for those who may get lost. 6. Champagne brunch. Mention food only if it's free or, for longer meetings and events, how it will be made available. Make it sound good, but don't overpromise. Let your surprises be pleasant ones. 7. Free admission and drawing. State the charges if there are any. For professional meetings that have a fee, be specific about what is covered and what will be provided. Be generous with the things that cost little (e.g., writing materials and note pads, outlines of presentations, tote bags, door prizes). Be equally specific about what attendees will pay for themselves (e.g., travel and lodging, specific meals, gratuities). Be mindful of possible legal problems with overly generous benefits. For example, a $500 luxury weekend for a $50 fee may raise questions later. Be prepared to document legitimate business necessities and off-season rates, or have advance approval from the appropriate attorney. 8. R.S.V.P. Make accepting the invitation easy. Include a reply card (and envelope for privacy). Encourage responses and questions by fax or phone. Have your reply form restate the major benefits, as well as any conditions of acceptance—especially those that favor the respondent. For example, a dieting program might read.

NOTES ON THE INVITATION/INVITATIONAL BULLETIN CHECKLIST These notes are a supplement to the material presented in this chapter. They are not a selfcontained substitute for that material. This checklist (Figure 4.6) covers the creation, printing, and mailing of invitations. It does not concern itself with who is invited or why, except insofar as that information (#6–7) must be reflected in the invitation. 1. Event Budget OK. Invitations generally take up only a small portion of an event's total cost. Has that complete budget been approved, and does it include the number of invitations you plan to use (#14)? If either answer is no, get written approval (#3) before you continue. 2. Quotations. Allow a week to get cost quotations and whatever time is required for their approval. On budgeted projects, these quotations should not have to go back to management for another round. 3. Invitation budget. If the budget as a whole has not been approved, can you get approval on the invitation portion? Give the decision makers absolute deadlines beyond which invitations are useless. 4. Speaker(s). Arrangements for speakers or other attractions or entertainment must generally be made far in advance of an event. Who decides? Who follows up? What's the last possible moment for including changes in the invitation? 5. Free/charges. What's free, and what costs, if any, will be charged to the participants? 6–7. Audience. Identify the audience to whom you are mailing the invitation and the specific focus of the invitation—the benefits, to the audience, of attending. 8–9. Copy. Identify the writer and designer of the invitation. Who follows whom? Who must approve the copy? When must both be done? 10. New art. Will there be hard copy produced by the designer or desktop publishing system? 11. New Art OK. Approval of final art is the last chance to make changes before the production of disk for film. Give an extra copy to those who must approve the original, for their notes and comments. 12. Proof OK. Approval of proofs is a combined design and advertising function, even when both are carried out by the same person. Design makes sure that the work has the quality specified on the art. Advertising makes sure that everything that was on the original is on the proof and that the designer's instructions still make sense when seen in print. If you do both jobs, wear one hat at a time, but be sure that both get worn. 13. Printing OK. For routine jobs, most printers can be left to their own devices. For large, complicated, or otherwise critical projects, be at the printer to give on-press approval. You'll be so bored that it will be the perfect time to read the entire copy one more time . . . and actually call all the telephone numbers and check on the addresses. About 10 percent. of the time, you'll be very glad you did! (I twice saved major projects by calling new toll-free numbers given to me by clients and about to be printed on every page of their catalogs, only to find them wrong.) 14. Quantity. The quantity is frequently more than the mailing list. Ask about nonmail distribution to staff and field workers and for last-minute follow-up

15. Mailing list. Who supplies the list, contacts the sources on the list, and checks to make sure that it is reasonably accurate? When using outside lists, responses only, not the list as a whole, become your property for future use. 16. Telephone list. Will you phone, fax, or e-mail to issue invitations or as a reminder to those who accept? For initial invitations, what is involved in getting the phone numbers and in getting through to those you call? Test by actually trying to call a dozen potential guests before you commit yourself to getting results. 17–18. Mail format. If you are using a self-mailer, skip #18 and #19. If you are using an envelope, check

with suppliers of envelopes regarding standard sizes and costs. It's seldom economical to customize envelopes for fewer than 10,000. Before you get too creative, check with the post office to make sure they'll accept the mail as designed. They almost always say yes, but check. 19. Components. Components include the invitation plus any other elements, such as RSVPs and reply envelopes. Don't be afraid to load up the invitation. If travel is involved, add a map. If the speaker is special, tell why. If the event is extraordinary, tell how. Use a separate invitationsize sheet for each of those items, and watch attendance soar! 20. Size. Invitation sizes are determined by the envelope. If the quantity is large so that you will use a mailing service (see Chapter 16), check with them about the practicality of inserting the invitations into the envelopes by machine. The envelope design is critical. Do this before anything, including the mailing list and how it will be addressed, is ordered. 21–22. Stock/Color. Not every paper stock comes in every color, especially when you want to match or contrast an envelope. But you can often print the stock into the color you want. It costs practically nothing extra when that color is a tint of a darker ink used on the same page. Discuss this with your prepress firm and printer. You may be pleasantly surprised. 23. Printing colors. Use any color paper and ink you wish—as long as the message can be read. If printed in light pink and blue or similar tones, your project may well die before the very eyes of those too nearsighted to see it. 24. Out date. The mailing date should be determined by considering the audience to whom you are sending the invitations. How booked up do they get for the time involved? How willing are they to commit their time far in advance? If you're not sure and can't easily find out, telephone a few invitees and ask. They will thank you for your concern! 25–26. In date. When must you have replies to permit final planning for the event? Telephone (#16) key prospects a few days before the deadline to reinvite them or to confirm their acceptance. There's nothing like an actual human voice to generate response. 27. Mail class. Most invitations are sent by first-class mail. Use a stamp or a printed permit that looks like a meter. For larger mailings, don't pre stamp the RSVP envelope. But just to play safe, test your level of response by adding a stamp to every tenth reply envelope. Let results guide future invitations. 28. Film supplier. For routine mailing pieces, your printer may wish to supply the film. Whether you agree or use a prepress firm, the proofing process (#12) is the same and is a production responsibility rather than an advertising decision. Where the two jobs are handled separately, thank those involved, and let them do their job. 29.

Printer. Printing is also a production function. For major projects, insist on being kept informed. For others, let those doing the job do it without your help. If you are a printing novice, ask them to help you learn. Don't pretend to expertise you don't have: You do not have to know how to fix something to insist on its being done right. 30. Mailing service. Your direct mail production company works on a schedule, too. Don't surprise them with projects out of the blue, or you may be blue indeed when you get the bill. Usually, anything can be done if you are willing to spend the money. Just remember . . . it is your money. Plan, stay on schedule, and save. 31. Records/Reports. What records must be kept? By whom? What analyses of results done? What reports made and to whom?

CHAPTER FIVE

Direct Mail and Database Direct Marketing

DIRECT MARKETING METHODS Direct magazine's 2002 analysis shows 19 methods to persuade or sell your prospects and customers through direct marketing. Though not all are in this chapter, they all are covered in this book. • Card packs • Fax marketing outbound • Catalogs • Freestanding inserts • CD-ROM marketing • Inbound telemarketing (including toll-free) • Co-op mailings • Interactive TV • Direct mail (noncatalog) • Internet1 • Direct response promotions • Outbound telemarketing/teleservicing • Direct response radio advertising • Package inserts • Direct response TV • Point of purchase • E-mail to prospects • Self-mailers • E-mail to customers • Trackable coupons This chapter has three goals: 1. To help you create your own direct response mailings. 2. To guide you in the supervision of mailings done by staff or outside experts. 3. To give you the basic rules and cautions for doing both.

The chapter begins with some basic rules and cautions about what is likely to work—and what isn't—in selling by mail. It continues with specific guidance on how to create a direct mail promotion—always keeping in mind those basic rules and cautions. Four of these will be absolutely critical to your success: 1. The single most important factor in selling by mail is the list. 2. Test whenever possible. Treat every mailing as a retest. 3. Believe the numbers. 4. Know the value of a customer, not just of the order.

TO CREATE OR SUPERVISE: WHEN TO DO EACH Of course, any project may be supervised rather than self-produced, depending on the time, budget, and talent available for it. If you have no skill for doing designs or layouts, employ others for those tasks, no matter how simple the project or how much time is available. Whether you do it yourself or supervise, here are some basic rules any design should follow: • Show and tell the readers what you are selling. If what you say and picture isn't absolutely clear, they won't guess. They won't buy! • Use type that's easy to read. The less sans serif, the easier it will be to read. • Keep it simple. The fancier the design, the more costly it will be to print it well. • "Flow-channel" your reader; that is, make sure that the mailing as a whole, and every piece in it, flows from an attention-grabbing beginning to an action-doing end. These and other such "rules" are found throughout this chapter. Use them when you do the job yourself. But equally important, insist on them when you turn work over to others. Do this before they begin, as part of your directions, not as expensive, time-consuming client's alterations after they've completed their initial copy and design. Make the rules part of your own checklist if they're not already included in the ones presented here. What You Must Not Do Yourself Two kinds of mailings must be created by direct mail professionals and should never be attempted as do-it-yourself "gifted amateur" projects: 1. A project, no matter how seemingly simple, that determines the survival of your business. (Of course you'll go to a specialist for a heart transplant, but will you try your own simple appendectomy?) 2. True direct mail "packages," such as multicomponent sweepstakes, giant "bedsheet" folded and refolded self-mailers, pop-up or other multidimensional projects. On any mailing that will cost more than $15,000, allow 20 percent for copy and design, and you'll probably be ahead in dollars and results. Good management includes learning to recognize the difference between getting something done exactly as you would do it yourself and having it done competently in some other way. Doing Your Own Mailings Help with creating your own mailings begins on page 90, but don't go there yet. The basics of lists, testing, and numbers that you must know for success, hold true no matter who does the mailing or what it costs. The next few pages explain them and how to apply them to what you write, design, and mail.

The single most important factor in selling by mail is the mailing list. According to a Dun & Bradstreet online report, other factors being equal, the list contributes 60 percent to the success of your mailing. Offer is given 20 percent; copy, 15 percent; and format (design, envelope, art treatment, etc.), 5 percent. The art and science of selecting lists lie in our ability to match the recipient with the offer—to mail only to those most likely to buy. No matter what we are selling—no matter how appealing the offer—if the recipient is not in the market for our products, nothing else matters. We're not going to sell dog food to cat fanciers; we're not going to sell chain saws to apartment-dwelling couch potatoes. From the marketers' standpoint, a mailing—as well as any other promotion—becomes junk when it is targeted at the wrong audience or when the quality of the mailing gives the wrong image of the sender. Note that the wrong image may be too rich as well as too poor! There is no better prospect than a satisfied customer. The most responsive mailing list is almost always made up of your present customers and clients, provided that such a list exists and that they have been well served in the past. That is why so many businesses use such ingenuity to gain your name and address when you pay by cash. You're their best prospect for mail order, too. When, however even your customer list seems to contain little useful information, some basic research is in order. People with like lifestyles tend to purchase alike. The key to selling is to determine which lifestyles match what you are offering. There are thousands of mailing lists available through list companies and brokers. (Chicago's business-to-business Yellow Pages list about 100 such companies.) The more we know about the meaningful characteristics of our current customers or clients, the easier it will be to find likely prospects by matching their customer profiles to ours. What's meaningful may not be a matter of common sense, so discuss with several mailing list professionals how they propose to help you find out and what they charge for their service. Then check the advice you get in a test mailing.

• Fewer than 5,000 names is not a statistically valid test. No matter how large the list, a 10,000-name test is almost always adequate. • For consumer lists, services exist that can match addresses with socioeconomic census data. Use the nth-name system of every 20th, 50th, or 500th name, depending on the size of your list, for a test mailing. You'll get a wealth of information on these people's lifestyles. • For business and professional lists, existing directories can tell you everything you need to know—from an individual's specialization, age, income, family, and automobiles owned to a corporation's history, profits, officers, and credit rating. If a certain piece of information seems pertinent, it's there for the matching. • A mailing list specialist, preferably experienced with your type of business, can help you analyze your lists. Before you request such help, get firm, written cost quotations and current references. Check them out! For New Businesses When your business is new, without customers or clients, there are four possibilities regarding mailing lists: 1. Lists exist to fill your needs. Your market is so well defined that available lists are all you need to get started. 2. Your market is hidden within a larger audience for which there are lists.

3. Lists exist, but they are not available to you. 4. No known list exists that will fill your needs. Let's consider each of these in more detail. Lists That Fit With lists that fit, your most important decision may seem to be whether to use the list as a whole or to start in with a test. But before you do either of these, check on the percentage of previous mail order buyers in that list, no matter what they have bought or what you are selling.2 Have the sources of the list give you those proven direct mail buyers only. (Forced subscriptions to association magazines and newsletters don't count.) It's almost always easier to sell such buyers a second time than to sell nonbuyers the first. If no list of previous buyers exists—and you feel that you must sell by mail—test! Lists That Hide Let's assume that you have a special racket for overweight, left-handed tennis players, but no mailing list exists for such individuals. A broader "umbrella" list of all tennis players, however, is available. Should you try to sell your submarket within it? The answer involves the same analysis you should do before any other mailing. Do as little blind guessing as possible. Do a market breakdown; that is, work with what you know or can learn—for instance, the percentage of left-handers in the general population and the degree of overweight seen at local tennis courts and clubs. Although this type of "knowing" is far from certain, it's better than sheer guesswork, and it lets you go to the next step: the calculation of testing costs and the application of test results as a predictor of complete mailings. A number of easy-to-use formulas exist for this purpose (see pages 105–107). Lists That Remain Private Many mailing lists are so valuable to their owners that they are never made available to anyone else. This is especially true of business customers and prospects, such as Collectibles for whom their list is their most valuable promotion property. General consumer lists tend to be less jealously guarded, for two reasons: 1. Increased use of a mailing list tends to build a larger universe of frequent buyers. As different kinds of products and services are offered, more recipients get into the habit of ordering by mail, making the list increasingly valuable as a source of proven mail-order buyers. 2. For many owners of a list, the income from renting the list is a major factor in their profitability. Suppose a list of 200,000 names generates net rental revenues of $25 per thousand 15 times a year. How much of the product would have to be sold to produce the same number of dollars in net income? The fact that some lists are not generally available tells you that people have been able to build them for themselves. If you have a list of your own, perhaps you can trade, rather than rent. If not, perhaps you can build your own

list, too. When No List Exists Even when no list exists for a particular market, it's probable that the names are there if only you can find a way to get at them. It is possible that no one else has previously wanted just those names badly enough to create a list. But it's more likely that gathering the list would have been too difficult or costly. When no list exists, test using other media, including the Internet, to generate leads or sell. When no list exists, think very hard about the practicality of making direct mail the key to your selling effort. Things to Know about Using Lists Eliminate Duplicate Mailings Where Practical When using more than one list, the possibility of duplicate mailings becomes increasingly likely. Through a computerized system called merge/purge, most of this duplication can be eliminated. But before deciding to use this program, discuss the process and costs with both a mailing list expert and a mailing service. Cost alone— lists, printing, mail handling, postage—may not be the key factor: Recipients may become so annoyed at receiving multiple copies of the same thing that they will consider it junk mail and pay no attention to it. Testing here, as elsewhere, will be the best way to discover what, if any, increase in response is achieved—at what cost—by merge/purge. Much more about this is in Chapter 16. Some Legal Limitations on the Use of Mailing Lists When using a list other than your own, the rental agreement almost always calls for one-time mailing use only. You may not copy the list or any part of it, or use it for any other purpose, unless agreed to in writing by the owner of the list. After testing, consider negotiating for multiple use of the most successful lists at reduced cost. Do not, however, pay for such multiple use in advance. First make sure the full mailing lives up to the promise of the test return. Rental lists are "seeded," that is, they include a few names specifically added to discover unauthorized use. Any response to your mailing, however, whether it is an order, an inquiry, the acceptance of a premium, or anything else, makes the respondent's name yours to use in the future. With many mailings, you justify their cost by gaining repeat customers, rather than one-time selling of a product or service. Customer or One-Time Buyer Know what you need to gain from mailing—one-time sales or long-term customers—and evaluate the results accordingly. But beware of paying for customers and then giving them a product or service that reduces them to one-time buyers, or budgeting for customers while having nothing more to sell. Direct response may be the one way of doing business where you can sometimes lose a little bit on each sale and then make it up in volume—but only if you also know how to play that tune.

Know what business you are in and your capabilities! THE ABSOLUTE NECESSITY FOR TESTING In direct mail, or any other kind of direct response advertising, the likelihood of getting things just right and most cost-effective on the very first try is quite small. We can, of course, and often do produce profitable mailings on just one try. But most cost-effective is most often the result of testing—a process that never stops in many direct mail organizations.

Before performing any test, decide which category will determine the outcome. Will it be percentage of response? Average order? Quantity of response?3 Cost per response? Quality of response? Something else? No matter which you pick, be sure to record and analyze all of these, especially the Q Concepts; that is, the relationship of quality to quantity of the response. Just because we don't get the answer we want doesn't mean that another answer isn't better.

In testing, the version ("package") that does best is called the control. Everything thereafter is controlled by (evaluated against) this package. Most of us tend to use "control" synonymously with "success." Its actual meaning is "the best results thus far," which are subject to change with every mailing.

A word of caution: When a test shows an extraordinary improvement over the existing control, do a retest with a larger portion of your list, if possible. Don't hesitate to change to a package that works better. Believe the numbers; just make sure that they aren't a one-time fluke.

Changing one or more factors in your mailings may give you a better response, but it may also have no effect or decrease returns. Even an increased response may have to be balanced against higher mailing costs, and lower costs may have to be balanced against fewer sales. It is quite common to test totally different mailing packages against each other—one or more quite expensive and the others somewhat plainer and less costly. But when testing to see whether a specific package can be made more effective, change only one thing if you wish to understand the results.

Because it takes a mailing of 5,0004 pieces to generate fairly predictable results, you will need 12 different mailings totaling 60,000 pieces for your test. The reason we need so many is that we are testing one specific factor in each mailing, yet testing that one factor against all the other 11: • Each of the prices is tested against all combinations of offers and colors. • Each of the color arrangements is tested against all combinations of offers and prices. • Each offer is tested against all combinations of colors and prices.

Should one of the offers be tested at random—for instance, the four-color offer A at $15.95 against the two-color offer B at $22.50—one will probably sell better than the other. But you have no way of knowing why—whether it was the offer or the price or the color that was responsible for the increased sales. Nor will you know which factor(s) you might change for even better results.

When to Stop Testing As you see in Figure 5.2, testing one more price will add 20,000 units for four more packages. Testing envelopes against self-mailers, or first-class postage against third-class postage, however, will double the number of units needed—from 60,000 to 120,000. You'll run out of names or money or both before you run out of tests, so let's take another look at testing. Five Ways to Approach Testing 1. Test everything. Test your product or service in exactly the way that was described in the last few pages. It's what the largest, most successful mailers do.

Test fewer than 5,000 names. When you really need to test how a large number of changes will influence results, and restrictions on budget, time, or names make testing 5,000 names impossible, test 2,000 names instead. Then take the top two or three results, and do a "real" test of 5,000 each. If you can possibly avoid it, don't go from a 2,000-name test to a "rollout"—a mailing of a much larger portion of your list or a complete mailing of the entire list. If you do not have time for a real test and results are important, either don't mail, or use a professional—and pray! 4. Use telemarketing to test before you mail. If your primary concern is your offer or price, give serious consideration to a telemarketing premailing test. Properly structured, it's fast, accurate, and the way to find out why someone doesn't buy, as well as why they do. (See Chapter 9 for a more detailed discussion of telemarketing for premail testing.) 5. Use print media to test before you mail. Find print media—magazines, newspapers, and newsletters—that go to the audience you want to reach. Check with each one to learn whether it accepts preprinted advertisements on postcardweight stock. You want the best results from your test, and a reply card almost always increases response. That card, in combination with a toll-free number, should give you the best results. If card stock is not acceptable but regular paper inserts are, consider an order form similar to what is used in most catalogs, preaddressed and, if publication policy permits, postage free. How to Prepare Your Print Media Test Let's use the 12 variables shown in Figure 5.2. Do the following: • Use a freestanding insert for your test. • Check with each publication on the size, format, and delivery date for your insert.

Newspapers will probably accept 8½ 11. Magazines not only vary in page size but usually require extra paper for trim. If unsure how to handle all this, get help from a printer experienced in this field or a print media production pro. • Prepare each test as an insert with all of the four-color or all of the twocolor offers printed together. If you are printing on postcard-weight stock, for easy removal, have the card edges perforated. • Use a department number to code each reply form. Use the same department codes for telephone response and add "M" for mail and "T" for telephone. Keep the system simple. If you're not staffed to handle telephone orders, see telemarketing services in Chapter 9. • After printing, have the 12 versions separated by your printer or bindery and collated sequentially, that is, into the order 1, 2, 3, 4 . . . 12. This gives you random, valid testing. What you must not permit is using all the #1's first, then all the #2's, and so on. Do not expect the percentage of response from a print media test that you would get from direct mail. If print gives you a clear winner and time and budget permit, test the winner in the mail against the two runners-up. Otherwise, use only the winner for the complete mailing. The least that you want to learn is the reliability of your print media testing. A word of warning: Many professional publications build their circulation by sending multiple copies to the same destination, although not often to the same person. Persons within the same organization will thus get different versions of your offer! If they compare and contact you about the differences, tell them you are running a test. They'll understand.

Various laws permit you to test different offers in the same mailing or advertisement. Check with the post office concerning current restrictions—if there are any—before testing. It is good business practice to fill all test responses at the lowest price being tested, no matter what the final price turns out to be. If that should be one of the higher prices, write the respondents who purchased with the lower prices in mind a thank-you note, and mention the price at which you will fill their orders in the future. If a lower price wins, congratulate those who purchased at the higher prices on recognizing value. Explain that the large volume of orders now permits a cost saving . . . and would they like to order some more at the unexpected saving!

CHAPTER SIX

A Sharp Pencil Works Best

IS THIS A GREAT JOB OR WHAT? As an employee in an agency creative department, you will spend most of your time with your feet up on a desk working on an ad. Across the desk, also with his feet up, will be your partner-in my case, an art director. And he will want to talk about movies. In fact, if the truth be known, you will spend a large part of your career with your feet up talking about movies. The ad is due in two days. The media space has been bought and paid for. The pressure's building. And your muse is sleeping off a drunk behind a dumpster or twitching in a ditch somewhere. Your pen lies useless. So you talk movies. That's when the traffic person comes by. Traffic people stay on top of a job as it moves through the agency. Which means they also stay on top of you. They'll come by to remind you of the horrid things that happen to snail-assed creative people who don't come through with the goods on time. So you try to get your pen moving. And you begin to work. And working, in this business, means staring at your partner's shoes. That's what I've been doing from nine to five for over 20 years. Staring at the bottom of the disgusting tennis shoes on the feet of my partner, parked on the desk across from my disgusting tennis shoes. This is the sum and substance of life at an agency. In movies, they almost never capture this simple, dull, workaday reality of life as a creative person. Don't get me wrong, it's not an easy job. In fact, some days it's almost painful coming up with good ideas. As author Red Smith said, "There's nothing to writing. All you do is sit down at a typewriter and open a vein."1 But the way movies show it, creative people solve complicated marketing problems between wisecracks and office affairs. Hollywood's agencies are always kooky sorts of places where odd things are nailed to or stuck on the walls, where weirdly dressed creative people lurch through the hallways metabolizing last night's chemicals, and the occasional goat wanders through in the background. But that isn't what agencies are like.

At least not the four or five agencies where I've worked. Again, don't get me wrong. An ad agency is not a bank. It's not an insurance company. There is a certain amount of joie de vivre in an agency's atmosphere. Which isn't surprising. Here you have a tight-knit group of young people, many of them making significant salaries just for sitting around with their feet up, solving marketing problems. And talking about movies. It's a great job because you'll never get bored. One week you'll be knee-deep in the complexities of the financial business, selling market-indexed annuities. The next, you're touring a dog food factory asking about the difference between a "kibble" and a "bit." You'll learn about the business of business by studying the operations of hundreds of different kinds of enterprises. The movies and television also portray advertising as a schlocky business—a parasitic lamprey that dangles from the belly of the business beast. A sort of side business that doesn't really manufacture anything in its own right, where it's all flash over substance, and where silver-tongued salespeople pitch snake oil to a bovine public, sandblast their wallets, and make the 5:20 for Long Island. Ten minutes of work at a real agency should be enough to convince even the most cynical that an agency's involvement in a client's business is anything but superficial. Every cubicle on every floor at an agency is occupied by someone intensely involved in improving the client's day-to-day business, in shepherding its assets more wisely, sharpening its business focus, widening its market, even improving the product. Ten minutes of work at a real agency should be enough to convince a cynic that you can't sell a product to someone who has no need for it. That you can't sell a product to someone who can't afford it. And that advertising can't save a bad product. In ten minutes the cynic will also see there's no back room where snickering airbrush artists paint images of breasts into ice cubes, no slush fund to buy hookers for the clients' conventions, and no big table in the conference room where employees have sex during the office Christmas party. (Um, scratch that last one.) Advertising isn't just some mutant offspring of capitalism. It's one of the main gears in the machinery of a huge economy, responsible in great part for one of the highest standards of living the world has ever seen. That Diet Coke you had an hour before you bought this book? It's just one of about 30,000 success stories of marketer and agency working together to bring a product—and with it, jobs and industry—to life. Diet Coke didn't just happen. Coca-Cola didn't simply roll it out and hope that people would buy it. Done poorly, they could have cannibalized their flagship brand, Coke. Done poorly, it could have been just another one of the well-intentioned product start-ups that fail in six months. It took a lot of work by both Coca-Cola and its agency, SSCB, to decipher market conditions, position the product, name it, package it, and pull off the whole billion-dollar introduction. Advertising, like it or not, is a key ingredient in a competitive economy and has created a stable place for itself in America's business landscape. Advertising is now a mature industry. And for most companies, a business necessity. Why most of it stinks remains a mystery. Carl Ally, founder of one of the great agencies of the 1970s, had a theory: "There's a tiny percentage of all the work that's great and a tiny percentage that's lousy. But most of the work—well, it's just there. That's no knock on advertising. How many great restaurants are there? Most aren't good or bad, they're just adequate. The fact is, excellence is tough to achieve in any field.

WHY NOBODY EVER CHOOSES BRAND X. There comes a point when you can't talk about movies anymore and you actually have to get some work done.

You are faced with a blank sheet of paper, and you must, in a fixed amount of time, fill it with something interesting enough to be remembered by a customer who in the course of a day will see, somewhere, thousands of other ad messages. You are not writing a novel somebody pays money for. You are not writing a sitcom somebody enjoys watching. You are writing something most people try to avoid. This is the sad, indisputable truth at the bottom of our business. Nobody wants to see what you are about to put down on paper. People not only dislike advertising, they're becoming immune to most of it—like insects building up resistance to DDT. The way Eric Silver put it was this: "Advertising is what happens on TV when people go to the bathroom." When people aren't indifferent to advertising, they're angry at it. If you don't believe me, go to the opening night of a big Hollywood movie. When the third commercial comes up on the screen and it's not the movie, those moans you hear won't be audience ecstasy. People don't want to see your stinkin' ad. Your ad is the comedian who comes on stage before a Rolling Stones concert. The audience is drunk and they're angry and they came to see the Stones. And now a comedian has the microphone? You had better be great. So you try to come up with some advertising concepts that can defeat these barriers of indifference and anger. The ideas you try to conjure, however, aren't done in a vacuum. You're working off a strategy—a sentence or two describing the key competitive message your ad must communicate. In addition to a strategy, you are working with a brand. Unless it's a new one, that brand brings with it all kinds of baggage, some good and some bad. Ad people call it a brand's equity. A brand isn't just the name on the box. It isn't the thing in the box, either. A brand is the sum total of all the emotions, thoughts, images, history, possibilities, and gossip that exist in the marketplace about a certain company. What's remarkable about brands is that in categories where products are essentially all alike, the best-known and most wellliked brand has the winning card. In The Want Makers, Mike Destiny, former group director for England's Allied Breweries, was quoted: "The many competitive brands [of beer] are virtually identical in terms of taste, color and alcohol delivery, and after two or three pints even an expert couldn't tell them apart. So the consumer is literally drinking the advertising, and the advertising is the brand." A brand isn't just a semantic construct, either. The relationship between the brand and its customers has monetary value; it can amount to literally billions of dollars. Brands are assets, and companies rightfully include them on their financial balance sheets. When you're writing for a brand, you're working with a fragile, extraordinarily valuable thing. Not a lightweight job. Its implications are marvelous. The ad you're about to do may not make the next million for the brand's marketer nor bring them to Chapter 11. Maybe it's just a half-page ad that runs one time. Yet it's an opportunity to sharpen that brand's image, even if just a little bit. It's a little like being handed the Olympic torch. You won't bear this important symbol all the way from Athens. Your job is just to move it a few miles down the road. Without dropping it in the dirt along the way .

STARING AT YOUR PARTNER'S SHOES. For me, writing an ad is unnerving. You sit down with your partner and put your feet up. You read the account executive's strategy, draw a square on a pad of paper, and you both stare at the damned thing. You stare at each other's shoes. You look at the square. You give up and go to lunch. You come back. The empty square is still there. So you both go through the product brochures and information folders the account team left in your office. Hmmm. You point out to your partner that this bourbon you're working on is manufactured in a little town with a funny name. Your partner looks out the window, stares at some speck in the distance, and says, "Oh." Down the hallway, a phone rings. Reading from the client's web site, your partner points out that the distillers rotate the aging barrels a quarter turn to the left every few months. You go, "Hmmm." You read that moss on trees happens to grow faster on the sides that face a distillery's aging house. That's interesting. You feel the glimmer of an idea move through you. You poise your pencil over the page. And it all comes out in a flash of creativity. (Whoa. Someone call 9-1-1. Report a fire on my drawing pad 'cause I am SMOKIN' hot.) You put your pencil down, smile, and read what you've written. It's complete rubbish. You call it a day and slink out to see a movie.

This process continues for several days, even weeks, and then one day without warning, an idea just shows up at your door, all nattied up like a Jehovah's Witness.You don't know where it comes from. It just shows up. That's how you come up with ideas. Sorry, there's no big secret. That's basically the drill. A guy named James Webb Young, a copywriter from the 1940s, laid out a five-step process of idea generation that holds water today. 1. You gather as much information on the problem as you can. You read, you underline stuff, you ask questions, you visit the factory. 2. You sit down and actively attack the problem. 3. You drop the whole thing and go do something else while your subconscious mind works on the problem. 4. "Eureka!" 5. You figure out how to implement your idea.4 Step two is what this book is about: attacking the problem. This process of creativity isn't just an aimless sort of blue-skying— a mental version of bad modern dance. Rather, it's what author Joseph Heller (a former copywriter) called "a controlled daydream, a directed reverie." It's imagination disciplined by a single-minded business purpose. So you start to write. Or doodle. (It doesn't matter which. Good copywriters can think visually; good art directors can write.) You just pick up a pencil and begin. All beginnings are humble, but after several days you begin to translate that flat-footed strategy into something interesting. The final idea may be a visual. It may be a headline. It may be both. It may arrive whole, like Athena arising out of Zeus's head. Or in pieces—a scribble made by the art director last Friday fits beautifully with a headline the writer comes up with over the weekend. Eventually you get to an idea that dramatizes the benefit of your client's product or service. Dramatizes is the key word. You must dramatize it in a unique, provocative, compelling, and memorable way.

If you want to be an award-winning copywriter, please yourself. If you want to be a great copywriter, please your reader."5 Here's the hard part. You have to please your reader and you have to do it in a few seconds. Paul Keye, a well-known West Coast creative, had a good way of putting this: "How to write an interesting ad? Try this: 'Hello. I want to tell you something important or interesting or useful or funny. It's about you. I won't take very long and there's a prize if you stay till the very end.'"6 The way I picture it is this: It's as if you're riding down an elevator with your customer. You're going down only 15 floors. So you have only a few seconds to tell him one thing about your product. One thing. And you have to tell it to him in such an interesting way that he thinks about the promise you've made as he leaves the building, waits for the light, and crosses the street. You have to come up with some little thing that sticks in the customer's mind. By "thing," I don't mean gimmick. Anybody can come up with an unrelated gimmick. Used car dealers are the national experts with their contrived sales events—"The boss went on vacation and our accountant went crazy!"—You might capture somebody's attention for a few seconds with a gimmick. But once the ruse is over and the salesman comes out of the closet in his plaid coat, the customer will only resent you. Bill Bernbach: "I've got a great gimmick. Let's tell the truth." The best answers always arise out of the problem itself. Out of the product. Out of the realities of the buying situation. Those are the only paints you have to make your picture, but they are all you need. Any shtick you drag into the situation that is not organically part of the product or customer reality will ring false. You have more than enough to work with, even in the simplest advertising problem. You have your client's product with its brand equities and its benefits. You have the competition's product and its weaknesses. You have the price-quality-value math of the two products.And then you have what the customer brings to the situation— pride, greed, vanity, envy, insecurity, and a hundred other human emotions, wants, and needs, one of which your product satisfies. THE SUDDEN CESSATION OF STUPIDITY. "You've got to play this game with fear and arrogance." That's one of Kevin Costner's better lines from the baseball

movie Bull Durham. I've always thought it had an analog in the advertising business. There has never been a time in my career I have faced the empty page and not been scared. I was scared as a junior-coassistant-copycub-intern. And I'm scared today. Who am I to think I can write something that will interest 10 million people? Then, a day after winning a medal in the One Show (just about the toughest national advertising awards show there is), I feel bulletproof. For one measly afternoon, I am an Ad God. The next day I'm back with my feet up on the table, sweating bullets again. Somewhere between these two places, however, is where you want to be—a balance between a healthy skepticism of your reason for living and a solar confidence in your ability to come up with a fantastic idea every time you sit down to work. Living at either end of the spectrum will debilitate you. In fact, it's probably best to err on the side of fear. A small, steady pilot light of fear burning in your stomach is part and parcel of the creative process. If you're doing something that's truly new, you're in an area where there are no signposts yet—no up and down, no good or bad. It seems to me, then, that fear is the constant traveling companion of an advertising person who fancies himself on the cutting edge. You have to believe that you'll finally get a great idea. You will. And there is nothing quite like the feeling of cracking a difficult advertising problem. What seemed impossible when you sat down to face the empty white square now seems so obvious. It is this very obviousness of a great idea that prompted Polaroid camera inventor, E.H. Land, to define creativity as "the sudden cessation of stupidity." You look at the idea you've just come up with, slap your forehead, and go, "Of course, it has to be this." "YOU LIKE ME.YOU REALLY LIKE ME." Solving a difficult advertising problem is a great feeling. Even better is the day, weeks or months later, when an account executive pops his head in your door and says sales are up. It never ceases to amaze me when that happens. Not that I doubt the power of advertising, but sometimes it's just hard to follow the thread from the scratchings on my pad all the way to a ringing cash register in, say, Akron, Ohio. Yet it works.

People generally deny advertising has any effect on them. They'll insist they're immune to it. And perhaps, taken on a person-byperson basis, the effect of your ad is indeed modest. But over time, the results are undeniable. It's like wind on desert sands. The changes occurring at any given hour on any particular dune are small. A grain here, a handful there. But over time, the whole landscape changes. Try this on: 1980—Absolut Vodka is a little nothing brand. Selling 12,000 cases a year. That's nothing. (I'm sure 6,000 of that was me.) Ten years and one campaign later, this colorless, nearly tasteless, and odorless product is the preferred brand, selling nearly 3 million cases a year. All because of the advertising (Figure 2.2). More anecdotal, but equally impressive, were the results of the trade campaign created to attract advertisers to the pages of Rolling Stone magazine. After Fallon McElligott's famous "Perception/ Reality" campaign was up and running (Figure 2.3), publisher Jann Wenner was reported as saying,"It was like someone came in with a wheelbarrow of money and dumped it on the floor." It's a great business, make no mistake. I see what copywriter Tom Monahan meant when he said, "Advertising is the rock 'n' roll of the business world."

BRAND = ADJECTIVE. Each brand has its own core value. Dan Wieden says it another way: Brands are verbs. "Nike exhorts, IBM solves, and Sony dreams." Even Mr. Whipple, as bad as he was, helped Charmin equal soft. This is an important point, and before we talk about strategy, it bears some discussion. People don't have time to figure out what your brand stands for. It is up to you to make your brand stand for something. The way to do it is to make your brand stand for one thing. Brand adjective. Everything you do with regard to advertising and design—whether it's creating the product or designing the web site—adheres to absolutely draconian standards of simplicity. Recently, I was on the phone with a client who works for a nationwide chain of grocery stores. This director of marketing mentioned in passing that the number of brands on the shelves in his stores had just passed 50,000. That's 50,000 brands competing for a customer's attention. 50,000. This number alone should take the spring from the step of any advertising person whose job it is to make the silhouette of a brand show up on a customer's radar. Until recently, it's been reasonable to assume that the way to make customers remember a brand is to differentiate it from its competitors: "The model of car we're selling has incredible styling and the other guy's brand doesn't." But your competition isn't just the other guy's car. When you sit down to do an ad, you are competing with every brand out there. You're competing with the 50,000 packaged-good brands on the shelves at the grocery store, as well as every other product and service and logo in the country. You're competing for attention with every TV commercial that has ever aired, with each billboard on every mile of highway, with the entire bandwidth across the radio, and every one of the 100 trillion pixels on the Web. All those other advertisers want a piece of your customer, and they're going to get it at your client's expense. Looked at from this perspective, through the teeming forest of brands vying for customers' attention, cutting through the clutter may require more than giving a sharp knife-edge to your brand. It calls for a big, noisy, smoking chain saw. But a kick-ass Super Bowl commercial isn't what I mean by a chain saw. The chain saw you need is simplicity. SIMPLE = GOOD. When you think about it, what other antidote to clutter can there possibly be except simplicity? Perhaps we should try cutting through the clutter with clutter that's extremely entertaining? Should we air clutter that tests well? Or clutter that wins awards or clutter with a big 800 number? I propose that the only possible antidote to clutter is draconian simplicity. Draconian simplicity involves stripping your brand's value proposition down to the bone and then again to the marrow, carving away until you get down to brand adjective. Make your brand stand for one thing. Pair it with one adjective. But which adjective? If you ask consumers in focus groups to talk about buying a car, with sufficient amounts of Dr Pepper and M&M's, they will amaze you with their complex analysis of the auto-buying process. I'm not kidding.These groups go on for hours, days. But if you ask a guy in a bar, "Hey, talk to me about cars," he'll break it down to a word— usually an adjective. "Yeah, gonna get me a Jeep. They're tough." Porsches, they're fast. BMWs perform. And Volvos, they're . . . what? If you said "safe," you've given the same answer I get from literally every person I've ever asked. Ever. In every speech I've ever given, anywhere around the world, when I ask audiences,"What does Volvo stand for?" I hear the same answer every time: "Safety." Audiences in Berlin, Los Angeles, Helsinki, Copenhagen, New York City all give the same answer.The money Volvo has spent on branding has paid off handsomely. Volvo has successfully spot welded that one adjective to their marque. And here's the interesting bit: In the past couple of years, Volvo hasn't even made it onto the top 10 list of safest cars on the market. So here's a brand that, having successfully paired its logo to one adjective, rides the benefit of this simple position in customers' minds long after its products no longer even merit the distinction. Such is the power of simplicity. The adjective you choose is key. Once it's married to a brand, divorce can be ugly. On the good side, once it's paired with the brand, that one square foot of category space is taken. If all the good adjectives are taken, don't settle for the second best. ("'Refreshing' is taken? Oh well . . . gimme 'Quenching.'") Second best won't be different enough. Try a polar opposite. Or consider a flanking move. In ketchup, the adjective everyone fought over for a long time was to be the "tomato-iest." Then one day Heinz came along claiming it was the "slowest," and sales went up—and stayed up. You can also try creating a whole new adjective that alters the playing field in your favor. (Axe cologne's "Bom Chicka Wah Wah" comes to mind.) The right adjective, the answer, will come out of the product. Or from your customers. Ask them. They know the answer. Find an adjective and stick to it. But it's the sticking to it that so many brands seem to have trouble with. The problem may be that, from a client's perspective, there are many things to admire about the product. "How can we narrow down our brand's value proposition to a word? Our product lasts longer, it's less expensive, it works better. All that stuff's important." Yes, those secondary benefits are important, and, yes, they have a place: in the brochures, on the packaging, or two clicks into the web site. All those other benefits will serve to shore up the aggregate value proposition of a brand, once customers try it. But what they're going to remember a brand for, the way they're going to file it on their desktops, is with a word. Find that word. You may argue that I have oversimplified here. And I have; I'll accept the criticism. Because I'm arguing for purism in an area where it's often impossible to think that way. Many brands simply do not lend themselves to such clean theoretical distinctions. But at least try; try to find that one word. You're going to thank me when it comes time to sit down and think up an ad.

BEFORE YOU PUT PEN TO PAPER. Before you do any new thinking, there's some background work to do. You won't be doing it alone, though. You'll have help from the people in account service. The account folks are the people in charge of an account at an agency. They analyze the market, study the competition, and arrange for and interpret the research. They formulate strategy, set budgets, and do a whole bunch of other stuff, some of it boring. They also help you present work to the client. Overall, they're the liaison between client and agency, explaining one to the other. Some account people are great, some so-so, and some bad. It will pay to hitch up with the smart ones as soon as you can. The good ones have the soul of a creative person and will share your excitement over a great ad. They're articulate, honest, and inspiring, and they have a better batting average at selling your work. Here are some things I've learned from the great account people I've worked with. Start by examining the current positioning of your product. There's a book called Positioning: The Battle for Your Mind, one I recommend with many caveats. (Though the strategic thinking of the authors is sound, I have many differences with them on the subject of creativity, which they declare irrelevant.) The authors, Ries and Trout, maintain that the customer's head has a finite amount of space in which to remember products. In each category, there's room for perhaps three brand names. If your product isn't in one of those slots, you must "de-position" a competitor to take its place. Before you start, look at the current positioning of your product. What positions do the competitors occupy? What niches are undefended? Should you concentrate on defining your client's position, or do some de-positioning of the competition? Do they have an adjective? What's your adjective? Get to know your client's business as well as you can. Bill Bernbach said, "The magic is in the product. . . . You've got to live with your product. You've got to get steeped in it. You've got to get saturated with it." The moral for writers and art directors is: Do the factory tour. I'm serious. Go if you get the chance. Ask a million questions. How is the product made? What ingredients does it have? What are their quality control criteria? Read every brochure. Read every memo you can get your hands on. You may find ideas waiting in the middle of a spec sheet ready to be transplanted kit-and-caboodle into an ad. Learn their business. Your clients are going to trust you more if you can talk to them about their industry in their terms. They'll quickly find you boring or irrelevant if all you can speak about with authority is Century Italic. Your grasp of the client's marketing situation has to be as well versed as any account executive's. There are no shortcuts. Know the client. Know their product. Know their market. It will pay off. Louis Pasteur said, "Chance favors the prepared mind." On the other hand, there's value in staying stupid. This dissenting opinion was brought to my attention by a great copywriter, Mark Fenske. Mark says, "Don't give into the temptation to take the factory tour. Resist. It makes you think like the client. You'll start to come up with the same answers the client does." Mark thinks, as many do, that keeping your "tabula" extremely "rasa" makes your thinking fresher. He may be right. There's also this to consider: When you're on the factory floor watching the caps get put on the bottles, you are a long way from the customer's reality. All the customer cares about is "What's in it for me?" Get to know the client's customers as well as you can. Once you get into the agency business, you'll meet another member on the team, a person called a planner. It's the job of planners to learn as much as they can about the client's customers and feed it back to both client and agency. Read everything your planners give you before putting pen to paper. Remember, most of the ads you do will be targeted to people outside your small social circle, people with whom you have no more in common than U.S. citizenship. Take farming. I've written TV commercials selling herbicides to soybean farmers, but what do I know about farming? As a kid, I couldn't even keep an ant farm alive a week after it arrived in the mail. Getting into the mind-set of a soybean farmer took plenty of work—lots of videotaped interviews and plenty of reading. Your account planners can give you piles of material to study. But don't just read it. Feel it. Take a deep breath and sink slowly into the world of the person you're writing to. Maybe you're selling a retirement community. You're talking to an older person. Someone living on a fixed income. Maybe they're worried about becoming dependent on their kids. It hurts when they get out of a chair. The idea of shoveling snow has dark-red cardiac overtones. How does it feel to be them? Ask to see the entire file of the client's previous advertising. The client or the account executives will have it somewhere. Study it. Maybe they tried something that was pretty cool, but they didn't do it right. How could you do it better? It will get your wheels turning. It'll also keep you from presenting ideas the client has already tried. Insist on a tight strategy. Creative director Norman Berry wrote: "English strategies are very tight, very precise. Satisfy the strategy and the idea cannot be faulted even though it may appear outrageous. Many . . . strategies are often too vague, too open to interpretation. "The strategy for this product is taste,' they'll say. But that is not a strategy. Vague strategies inhibit. Precise strategies liberate."7 Poet T.S. Eliot never worked at an ad agency, but his advice about A Sharp Pencil Works Best 31 15934_Sullivan_c02_3p.r.qxp 1/2/08 10:05 AM Page 31 strategy is right on the money: "When forced to work within a strict framework, the imagination is taxed to its utmost and will produce its richest ideas. Given total freedom, the work is likely to sprawl." Dude nailed it. You need a tight strategy. On the other hand, a strategy can become too tight. When there's no play in the wheel, an overly specific strategy demands a very narrow range of executions and becomes by proxy an execution itself. Good account people and planners can fine-tune a strategy by moving it up and down a continuum that ranges between broad, meaningless statements and little purse-lipped creative dictums masquerading as strategies. When you have it just right, the strategy should be evident in the campaign but the campaign should not be evident in the strategy. Jean-Marie Dru put it elegantly in his book Disruption: There are two questions that need to be asked. The first is: Could the campaign I'm watching have been created without the brief? If the answer is yes, the odds are that the campaign is lacking in content. You have to be able to see the brief in the campaign. The second question is a mirror image of the first. . . . Is the campaign merely a transcription of the brief? If the answer is yes, then there has been no creative leap, and the campaign lacks executional force.7 Ultimately, a good strategy is inspiring. You can pull a hundred rabbits out of the same hat, creating wildly different executions all on strategy. Goodby, Silverstein & Partners' magnificent "milk deprivation" strategy called forth a long string of wonderful "Got milk?" executions.* Insist on a tight strategy. Will you always get one? No. In fact, in this business, they sometimes seem to be the exception, not the rule. But you must push for one as hard as you can. The final strategy should be simple. Advertising, as my friend Mark says, isn't "rocket surgery." People live and think in broad strokes. Like we said earlier, ask some guy in a mall about cars. He'll tell you Volvos are safe, Porsches are fast, and Jeeps are rugged. Boom. Where's the genius here? There isn't.

You want people who feel X about your product to feel Y. That's about it. We're talking one adjective here. Most of the time, we're talking about going into a customer's brain and spot welding one adjective onto a client's brand. That's all. DeWalt tools are tough. Coke is refreshing. I'm reminded of how Steven Spielberg said he preferred movie ideas that could be summed up in a sentence. "Lost alien befriends lonely boy to get home." The moral is: Keep it simple. Don't let the account executives or the client make you overthink it. Try not to slice too thin. Think in bright colors. Make sure what you have to say matters. It must be relevant. It must matter to somebody, somewhere. It has to offer something customers want or solve a problem they have, whether it's a car that won't start or a drip that won't stop. If you don't have something relevant to say, tell your clients to put their wallets away. Because no matter how well you execute it, an unimportant message has no receiver. The tree falls in the forest. Testing strategy is better than testing executions. This is the best of all possible worlds, and the day hell freezes over, all clients will be testing this way. A few do this now. Here's how it works. You sit down with the client, the planners, and the account team. You explore all the possible strategies available to your brand. You settle on 5 or 6—10, if you want. Then you make what are called "benefit boards." Simple, flatfooted layout things that look and feel like ads but aren't. Usually a picture with a headline that spells out with little fanfare exactly the strategy you'd like to test. For example, say the client manufactures aspirin. The pictures could be anything really—a shot of a person nursing a headache or a close-up of two aspirins on a tabletop. Next to the picture on each board is a headline pitching a different angle on the product: "Faster-acting Throbinex." "Throbinex is easy on the stomach." "Smaller, easier-to-swallow pills." Just crank them out. These aren't ads. They're benefits. Show 10 different boards like these to a focus group and you'll come away with a good idea of which messages resonate with customers. It's a great place to start. In fact, it's the only place to start. Go to the focus groups. Every chance you get to hear what customers are saying, take it. If there's a web site or chat room about a product or brand, go there. Eavesdropping is the best way to learn what customers think. Less useful (and usually more infuriating) is to hear what customers are saying about your work—in focus groups. I used to hate doing this; I still do. There are few things I hate more than listening to focus group people complain about my ideas.* I think pretesting concepts by showing rough layouts and storyboards to people off the street is a bane to the industry. (But more on that later, in Chapter 11.) For now, I say go to the groups, if only for the reason that it helps you sell work to the client. Because once you've put in the hours at the groups, you can say, "Yes, I sat there and stared through the glass at those people. I think I have a very good idea of what strategies work, what they like, and what they don't, and in my opinion this campaign will work." Read the publications your ads will be in. Check out the articles. See what your target customer is reading. Case the joint. Get a feel for the place your ad will be appearing. Read the awards books. Take a little inspiration from the excellence you see there. Then get ready to do something just as great.The best awards books are from the One Show and Communication Arts, as well as the British D&AD annuals. There are also the ad sites online. (I list several of the better ad sites in the back of this book, but keep in mind that they come and go.)

CHAPTER SEVEN

A Clean Sheet of Paper

LET'S BEGIN THIS PART OF OUR DISCUSSION with a quotation from Helmut Krone, the man who did what I think is the industry's first good ad: "I start with a blank piece of paper and try to fill it with something interesting." So if I'm working on a print ad, that's what I do. I get a clean sheet of paper and draw a small rectangle. I figure if an idea doesn't work in a small space, it's not going to work. And then I start. SAYING THE RIGHT THING THE RIGHT WAY. Remember, you have two problems to solve: the client's and yours. Imagine this circle is the target's bull's-eye of what the brand stands for. Any ad you do that lands inside this area is perfect. The client will love it. If it's outside the circle, they won't. Nor should they.

If your idea lands inside the client's brand space, they'll love it. If not, buh-bye.

The one on the left is the client's bull's-eye and on the right is the bull's-eye for what you think is a great ad. The trick is to hit that sweet spot where the two circles overlap. You solve the account team's and the client's problem by saying exactly the right thing. That's relatively easy; it's the strategy. But you aren't finished until both problems are solved. By nailing the sweet spot. Bernbach once said, "Dullness won't sell your product, but neither will irrelevant brilliance." Here, dullness is represented on the far left side of the left circle, and irrelevant brilliance on the far right side of the right. The moral? Do both perfectly. Hit the overlap. 38 "Hey, Whipple, Squeeze This" Figure 3.2 If your idea lands inside the client's brand space, they'll love it. If not, buh-bye. Figure 3.3 If your idea is only in the left circle, it might be boring. Only on the right, it might be stupid. Hit the sweet spot to win cash and prizes. 15934_Sullivan_c03_3p.r.qxp 1/2/08 10:06 AM Page 38 Pose the problem as a question. Creativity in advertising is problem solving. When you state the problem as a bald question, sometimes the answers suggest themselves. Take care not to simply restate the problem in the terms in which it was brought to you; you're not likely to discover any new angles. Pose the question again and again, from entirely different perspectives. In his book The Do-It-Yourself Lobotomy, Tom Monahan puts it this way: "Ask a better question." By that he means a question to which you don't know the answer. He likens it to "placing the solution just out of your reach," and in answering it, you stretch yourself.1 As philosopher John Dewey put it: "A problem well-stated is a problem half-solved." It can work. Eric Clark reminds us just how it works in his book The Want Makers. In the 1960s, a team wrestled for weeks for an idea to illustrate the reliability of the Volkswagen in winter. Eventually they agreed that a snowplow driver would make an excellent spokesman. The breakthrough came a week later when one of the team wondered aloud, "How does the snowplow driver get to his snowplow?"2 If you've never seen it, the VW "snowplow" commercial is vintage Doyle Dane. A man gets in his Volkswagen and drives off through deep snow into a blizzard. At the end, we see where he's driving: the garage where the county snowplows are parked. The voice-over then asks, "Have you ever wondered how the man who drives a snowplow . . . drives to the snowplow? This one drives a Volkswagen. So you can stop wondering." Don't be afraid to ask dumb questions. That blank slate we sometimes bring to a problem-solving session can work in our favor. We ask the obvious questions that people too close to the problem often forget. In the question's very naïveté, we sometimes find simple answers that have been overlooked. Ask yourself what would make you want to buy the product. A simple enough piece of advice and one I often forget about while I'm busy trying to write an ad. Sit across from yourself at your desk. A Clean Sheet of Paper 39 15934_Sullivan_c03_3p.r.qxp 1/2/08 10:06 AM Page 39 Quiet your mind. And ask, "What would make me want to buy this product?" Then try the flip side: What would you do if you were the one bankrolling the campaign? There was a writer at my agency who was also an investor in a new product—some kind of running gear. He was both the writer and the client. When he sat down to do ads for a company whose failure would cost him a significant amount of money, he saw how some of the things he hated hearing from clients had merit. Copywriter John Matthews wrote, "You learn a lot more about poker when you play for money and not for chips." Find the central truth about your product. Find the central truth about your whole product category. The central human truth. Hair coloring isn't about looking younger. It's about self-esteem. Cameras aren't about pictures. They're about stopping time and holding life as the sands run out. There are ads to be written all around the edges of any product. But get to the ones written right from the essence of the thing. In Hoopla, Alex Bogusky is talking about this essence when he says, "We try to find that long-neglected truth in a product and give it a hug."3 Notice he says they "find" this truth, not invent it. Roy Spence of GSD&M hits on the same point when he says, "Visionary ideas are discovered, not created." They're discovered. The best 40 "Hey, Whipple, Squeeze This" Figure 3.4 The headline could have been something boring like: "We're proud of our wide variety of beautiful flower arrangements. One's just right for your budget." 15934_Sullivan_c03_3p.r.qxp 1/2/08 10:06 AM Page 40 ideas are old truths brought to light in fresh, new ways. As an example, check out this ad by my friend Dean Buckhorn for the American Floral Marketing Council (Figure 3.4). He could have done something about how "purdy" flowers are. He didn't, and instead focused on one of the central human truths about this category—the use of flowers as a ticket out of the Casa di Canine. Try the competitor's product. What's wrong with it? More important, what do you like about it? What's good about their advertising? Then try this trick. In Marketing Warfare, Ries and Trout suggested, "Find a weakness in the leader's strength and attack at that point."4 A good example comes to mind, again from the pens of Bernbach's crew. Avis Rent A Car was only number two. So Avis suggested you come to them instead of Hertz because "The line at our counter is shorter." Dramatize the benefit. Not the features of the product, but the benefit those features provide the user, or what some call "the benefit of the benefit."There is an old advertising maxim that expresses this wisdom in a way that's hard to improve: "People don't buy quarter-inch drill bits. They buy quarter-inch holes." Avoid style; focus on substance. Remember, styles change; typefaces and design and art direction, they all change. Fads come and go. But people are always people. They want to look better, to make more money; they want to feel better, to be healthy. They want security, attention, and achievement. These things about people aren't likely to change. So focus your efforts on speaking to these basic needs, rather than tinkering with the current visual affectations. Focus first on the substance of what you want to say. Then worry about how. Make the claim in your ad something that is incontestable. Make it something that can't be argued about. Facts can't be refuted. There are some products to which this advice won't apply. A Clean Sheet of Paper 41 15934_Sullivan_c03_3p.r.qxp 1/2/08 10:06 AM Page 41 Products that are all image. Or products with no real difference worth hanging your hat on, like, I don't know, paper clips. But when you have a fact at your command, use it. When you can say, "This product lasts 20 years," what's to argue with? State fact, not manufactured nonsense about, oh, say, how "We Put the 'Qua' in Quality." GET SOMETHING, ANYTHING, ON PAPER. The artist Nathan Oliveira wrote, "All art is a series of recoveries from the first line. The hardest thing to do is put down the first line. But you must." Here are some ideas to help you get started. First, say it straight. Then say it great. To get the words flowing, sometimes it helps to simply write out what you want to say. Make it memorable, different, or new later. First, just say it. Try this. Begin your headline with: "This is an ad about . . ." And then keep writing. Who knows? You might find, by the time you get to the end of a sentence, you have something just by snipping off the "This is an ad about" part. Even if you don't, you've focused. A good first step. Whatever you do, just start writing. Don't let the empty page (what Hemingway called "the white bull") intimidate you. Go for art later. Start with clarity. Restate the strategy and put some spin on it. Think of the strategy statement as a lump of clay. You've got to sculpt it into something interesting to look at. So begin by taking the strategy and saying it some other way, any way. Say it faster. Say it in English. Then in slang. Shorten it. Punch it up. Try anything that will change the strategy statement from something you'd overhear in an elevator at a sales convention to a message you'd see spray painted on an alley wall. Club Med's tagline could have been "A Great Way to Get Away." It could have been "More Than Just a Beach." Fortunately, Ammirati & Puris had the account, and it became: "Club Med. The Antidote for Civilization."

Be careful, too, not to let your strategy show. Many ads suffer from this transparence, and it happens when you fail to put enough creative spin on the strategy. Your ad remains flat and obvious, there's no magic to it, and reading it is a bit of a letdown. It's like Dorothy discovering that the Wizard of Oz is just some knucklehead behind a curtain. In his book Disruption, Jean-Marie Dru described this kind of ad: You can tell when ads are trying too hard. Their intentions are too obvious. They impose themselves without speaking to you. By contrast, there are some that grab your attention with their executional brio, but their lack of relevance is such that after you've seen them they leave you kind of empty. Great advertising combines density of content with the elegance of form.5 Density of content and elegance of form. Great advice. What's the mood you want your reader or viewer to feel? This is a decision you can sometimes make early on in the process. It's likely based on the kind of product you are working with.

If you're working on a web site for a hospital, well, pie-in-the-face humor probably shouldn't be on the list of likely solutions. Pick a mood. A feeling. You can change your mind later, but sometimes it helps give you focus when you decide, "Okay, this campaign is gonna be . . . thoughtful." Or angry, or stark, or . . . well, you decide. What's right for your client? What's right for the customer? Allow yourself to come up with terrible ideas. In Bird by Bird, her book on the art of writing fiction, Anne Lamott says: The only way I can get anything written at all is to write really, really crappy first drafts. That first draft is the child's draft, where you let it pour out and then let it romp all over the place, knowing that no one is going to see it and that you can shape it later. You just let this childlike part of you channel whatever voices and visions come through and onto the page. If one of the characters wants to say, "Well, so what, Mr. Poopy Pants?," you let her.6 Same thing in advertising. Start with "Free to qualified customers" and go from there. A Clean Sheet of Paper 43 15934_Sullivan_c03_3p.r.qxp 1/2/08 10:06 AM Page 43 Remember, notebook paper is not made only for recording gems of transcendent perfection. A sheet of paper costs about onesquillionth of a cent. It isn't a museum frame. It's a workbench. Write. Keep writing. Don't stop. Allow your partner to come up with terrible ideas. The quickest way to shut down your partner's contribution to the creative process is to roll your eyes at a bad idea. Don't. Even if the idea truly and most sincerely blows, just say, "That's interesting," scribble it down, and move on. Remember, this is not a race. (Well, if it is, it's one of those nerdy three-legged races at the company picnic where you and your partner win or lose together.) You are not in competition with your partner. You are competing with your client's rival brands. No matter what your partner says, see if you can take it and shape it and mold it. Then throw it back to him or her with your idea tacked on. In a wonderful book called Creative Advertising, author Mario Pricken likens this conceptual back-and-forth to a game: " . . . a kind of ping-pong ensues, in which you catapult each other into an emotional state resembling a creative trance."7 Feed a baby idea lots of milk and burp it regularly. Nurture a newly hatched idea. Until it grows up, you don't know what it's going to be. So don't look for what's wrong with a new idea, look for what's right. And no playing the devil's advocate just yet. Instead, do what writer Sydney Shore suggests: Play the "angel's advocate." Coax the thing along. Share your ideas with your partner, even the kinda dumb half-formed ones. Just because an idea doesn't work yet, it might work eventually. I sometimes find I get something that looks like it might go somewhere, but I can't do anything with it. It just sits there. Some wall inside prevents me from taking it to the next level. That's when my partner scoops up my miserable little half-idea and runs with it over the goal line. Remember, the point of teamwork isn't to impress your partner by sliding a fully finished idea across the conference room table. It's about how 1 1 3. 44 "Hey, Whipple, Squeeze This" 15934_Sullivan_c03_3p.r.qxp 1/2/08 10:06 AM Page 44 That said, I feel the need to remind you not to say aloud every stinking thing that comes into your head. It's counterproductive. I worked with someone like this once, and I ended up with a bad case of "idea-rrhea" that lasted the whole weekend. Spend some time away from your partner, thinking on your own. I know many teams who actually prefer to start that way. It gives you both a chance to look at the problem from your own perspective before you bring your ideas to the table. Let your subconscious mind do it. Where do ideas come from? I have no earthly idea. Around 1900, a writer named Charles Haanel said true creativity comes from "a benevolent stranger, working on our behalf." Novelist Isaac Singer said, "There are powers who take care of you, who send you patience and stories." And film director Joe Pytka said, "Good ideas come from God." I think they're probably all correct. It's not so much our coming up with great ideas as it is creating a canvas where a painting can appear. So do what Marshall Cook suggests in his book Freeing Your Creativity: "Creativity means getting out of the way. . . . If you can quiet the yammering of the conscious, controlling ego, you can begin to hear your deeper, truer voice in your writing. . . . [not the] noisy little you that sits out front at the receptionist's desk and tries to take credit for everything that happens in the building."8 Stop the chatter in your head. Go into Heller's "controlled daydream." Breathe from your stomach. If you're lucky, sometimes the ideas just begin to appear. What does the ad want to say? Not you, the ad. Shut up. Listen. In The Creative Companion, David Fowler says, "Maybe if you walked around the block you could hear it more clearly. Maybe if you went and fed the pigeons they'd whisper it to you. Maybe if you stopped telling it what it needed to be, it would tell you what it wanted to be. Maybe you should come in early, when it's quiet."9 Try writing down words from the product's category. Most of the creative people I know have their own special system for scribbling down ideas. Figure out what works for you. For A Clean Sheet of Paper 45 15934_Sullivan_c03_3p.r.qxp 1/2/08 10:06 AM Page 45 me—let's say we're selling outboard engines—I start a list on the side of the page: Fish. Water. Pelicans. Flotsam. Jetsam. Atlantic. Titanic. Ishmael. What do these words make you think of? Pick up two of them and put them together like Tinkertoys. You have to start somewhere. Sure, it sounds stupid. The whole creative process is stupid. It's like washing a pig. I'm serious. It's exactly like washing a pig. It's messy; it has no rules, no clear beginning, middle, or end; it's kind of a pain in the ass, and when you're done, you're not sure if the pig is clean or even why you were washing a pig in the first place. Welcome to the creative department. Stare at a picture that has the emotion of the ad you want to do. Have you ever tried to write an angry letter when you weren't angry? Oh, you manage to get a few cusswords on paper, but there's no fire to it.The same can be said for writing a good ad.You need to be in the mood. I once had to do some ads for a new magazine called Family Life. The editors said this wasn't going to be just another "baby magazine," which are very much like diapers—soft, fluffy, and full of . . . My point is, they wanted ads that captured the righteous emotion of the editorial. Raising a child is the most moving, most important thing you'll ever do. To get in the mood, I did two things. I reread a wonderful book by Anna Quindlen on the joys and insanities of parenting called Living Out Loud. I'd soak up a couple of pages before I sat down to write.When I was ready to put pen to paper, I propped up a number of different stock photos of children, including a picture of a child in a raincoat, sitting in a puddle (Figure 3.5). As you can see in the ad reprinted here, the idea didn't come directly out of the photo, but in a way it did. It's worked for me. You might want to try it. Explore Jim Aitchison's format:"Do I want to write a letter or send a postcard?" In his book Cutting Edge Advertising, 10 Aitichison offers up this early fork in the road. Do you want to write a letter or just drop a postcard?

A postcard, says Aitchison, is an ad that's visually led. A single visual and a small bit of copy are all that are needed to make the point. For example, to get across the spirit and drive of the new Beetle,Arnold Communications did this simple postcard (Figure 3.6): "0–60? Yes." On the other hand, a letter is an ad that's predominantly copydriven. It's probably better for ads that have to deliver a more complex message. Just the sheer weight of the body copy adds a sense of gravitas to the product regardless of whether the consumer reads a word of the copy. Check out the beautiful ad for Land Rover done by my friends at GSD&M (Figure 3.7). There are both letter ads and postcard ads throughout this book. Take a look at how each visual or verbal format serves the different messages the brands are trying to convey. Find a villain. Find a bad guy you can beat up in the stairwell. Every client has an enemy, particularly in mature categories, where growth has to come out of somebody else's hide. Your enemy can be the other guy's scummy, overpriced product.

It can also be some pain or inconvenience the client's product spares you. If the product's a toothpaste, the villain can be tooth decay, the dentist, the drill, or that little pointy thing Laurence Olivier used on Dustin Hoffman in Marathon Man. ("Is it safe?") A villain can come from another product category altogether, in the form of what's called an indirect competitor. Parker Pens, for example, could be said to have an indirect competitor in word processors. A gracefully raised knee to a villain's groin isn't just fun, it's profitable. Because competitive positioning is implicit in every villain paradigm. It's also an easy and fun place from which to write. Mom was always telling us about "constructive criticism."Yeah, well highly underrated and much more fun is the concept of "destructive criticism." "Tell the truth and run." This old Yugoslavian proverb is a reminder of the power of truth. Even if you have an unpleasant truth, say it. "We're Avis. We're only number two. So we try harder." Totally believable. More important, I like a company that would say this about themselves. America loves an underdog. Perhaps the biggest underdog of all time was Volkswagen. VW was the king of self-deprecation. The honest voice Doyle Dane Bernbach created for this odd-looking little car turned its weaknesses into strengths.

Does the medium lend itself to your message? Some great ads have been done playing off of the very place they appear. This is well-tilled ground, so take care that your idea hasn't been done a hundred times before. But when it works, it works. The ad from Australia's Taronga Zoo is a great example and is reprinted at actual size (Figure 3.9). Be provocative. Sometimes the best way to bring the message home is to gallop into town and splash mud all over decent citizens. Provocative is good. It gets your client talked about. Go over the line once in a while, when it seems right. Just a couple of steps. Going way over the line may backfire on you.And please, don't take this as permission to do a "pee-pee" joke. If I see even one more ad with a sly nudge-nudge-wink-wink reference to penises, I think I shall retire to my chambers, close the door, and gently weep until dusk. Remember, being provocative just because you can isn't the point. Like Bernbach said, "Be sure your provocativeness stems from your product." This ad for the truth® youth-smoking prevention campaign qualifies (Figure 3.10). Here's a client that wants to use the natural rebellious tendencies of teenagers and turn them on the lies of tobacco companies. It's exactly the right time to pull out all the stops. "DO I HAVE TO DRAW YOU A PICTURE?" Be visual and go short on the copy. The screen saver on the computers at London's Bartle Bogle Hegarty reads, "Words are a barrier to communication." Creative director (CD) John Hegarty says, "I just don't think people read ads." I don't think most people read ads, either—at least not the body copy. There's a reason they say a picture is worth a thousand words. When you first picked up this book, what did you look at? I'm betting it was the pictures. Granted, if you interest readers with a good visual or headline, yes, they may go on to read your copy. But the point is, visuals work fast. As the larger brands become globally marketed, visual solutions will become even more important. They translate, not surprisingly, better than words. Visual solutions are so universal, they work even after years in a deep freeze. Look at the 1879 ad for the Diebold Safe & Lock Company of Cleveland, Ohio (Figure 3.11). Putting aside the issue of whether this is a good ad or not, I'll bet it's a lot better than any verbal equivalent from other safe manufacturers of the times. ("Doers of Evil and Kriminal Minds agree, Monies safekept in an Acme Vault are ne'er Pilfered For Gambling & Likker.") The ad for Mitsubishi's Space Wagon (Figure 3.12) from Singapore's Ball Partnership is one of my all-time favorites.The message is delivered entirely with one picture and a thimbleful of words. What could you possibly add to or take away from this concept? Relying on one simple visual means it assumes added responsibilities and a bigger job description. You can't bury your main selling idea down in the copy. If readers don't get what you're trying to say from the visual, they won't get it. The page is turned. Don't take my word for it. Watch someone in the airport read a magazine. They whip through, usually backward, at about two sec onds per page. They glance at the clock on the wall. They turn a page. They think about the desperate, pimpled loneliness of their high school years. They look at a page. They see your ad. If you can get them to take in your visual (or read your headline), your ad is a resounding success. Break out the Champale. Call your parents. You are a genius. Coax an interesting visual out of your product. One day when he was a little boy, my son Reed and I went through this mental exercise using his toy car. I held the car in its traditional four-wheels-to-the-ground position and asked him, "What's this?" "A car," he said. I tipped it on its side. Two wheels on the ground made the image "a motorcycle." I tipped the car on its curved top. He saw a hull and said, "Boat." When I set it tailpipe to ground, pointing straight up, he saw propulsion headed moonward and told me, "It's a rocket!" Look at your product and do the same thing. Visualize it on its side. Upside down. Make its image rubber. Stretch your product visually six ways to Sunday, marrying it with other visuals, other icons, and see what you get—always keeping in mind you're trying to coax out of the product a dramatic image with a selling benefit. What if it were bigger? Smaller? On fire? What if you gave it legs? Or a brain? What if you put a door in it? What is the wrong 54 "Hey, Whipple, Squeeze This" Figure 3.12 Long-copy ads can be great. This is not one of them. 15934_Sullivan_c03_3p.r.qxp 1/2/08 10:06 AM Page 54 way to use it? How else could you use it? What other thing does it look like? What could you substitute for it? Take your product, change it visually, and by doing so, dramatize a customer benefit. Get the visual clichés out of your system right away. Certain visuals are just old. Somewhere out there is a Home for Tired Old Visuals. Sitting there in rocking chairs on the porch are visuals like Uncle Sam, a devil with a pitchfork, and a proud lion, just rocking back and forth waiting for someone to use them in an ad once again. And grousing, "When we were young, we were in all kinds of ads. People used to love us." Remember: Every category has its own version of Tired Old Visuals. In insurance, it's grandfathers flying kites with grandchildren. In the tech industries, it's earnest people looking at computer screens. And in beer, it's boobs. Learn what iconography is overused in your category, and avoid it. Check out the ad for Polaris watercraft in . It's just a wild guess, but I'm thinkin' this is probably the first use of a hippo in the Jet Ski category.

Telling readers why your product has merit is never as powerful as showing them. I could take all day explaining how well a certain brand of vacuum cleaner works, but you'll sit up and take notice when I plug it in and show how it empties a sandbox in under a minute. Showing the benefit of your product also allows readers to reach their own conclusions. It's more involving. This great ad by BMP in London for Fisher-Price's antislip roller skates (Figure 3.14) is a good example of the benefits of showing your story, not telling it. It's one of my all-time favorites. Saying isn't the same as being. This is a corollary to the previous point. If a client says, "I want people to think our company is cool," the answer isn't an ad saying, "We're cool." The answer is to be cool. Nike never once said, "Hey, we're cool." They just were cool. C'mon, think about it. The Beatles didn't meet in the third-floor conference room and go over a presentation about how they were going to become known as cool. They just were cool. The folks at Crispin Porter Bogusky think the same way, focusing often on what they call "proof points." As an example, for their 56 "Hey,

Whipple, Squeeze This" Figure 3.14 The mental image this ad paints of two kids landing on their duffs is more powerful than actually showing them that way. 15934_Sullivan_c03_3p.r.qxp 1/2/08 10:06 AM Page 56 auto client MINI Cooper they could have run a TV commercial that said, "Hey America, this is one unconventional car that puts the fun back in driving!" Instead, they mounted a MINI on top of an SUV (typically the space you strap down the fun stuff like bikes and surfboards) and drove the hulking gas-guzzler around town with a message that said, "What are you doing this weekend?" The damn car fit up there. And when you saw this thing drive by you on the street, it was more than just a claim of unconventionality and fun. It was proof. As Miss Manners politely points out, "It is far more impressive when others discover your good qualities without your help." "THE REVERSE SIDE ALSO HAS A REVERSE SIDE." When everybody else is zigging, you should zag. There was this really dumb supervillain in the old Superman comics, Bizzaro-Man. He did everything . . . opposite. It was really stupid (and cool). Try being Bizzaro-Man. If your product is white sheets, write the headlines in mud. If your product is beautiful, show something ugly. If your product is an insurance ad, design it like a poster for a rock concert. Try writing your copy backward. Encircle the logo for your bank client with hot dogs. I'm not saying all this Bizzaro crap makes your idea great. But you should at least search as far outside the boundaries of convention as you can. It's likely you'll end up pulling back a bit, but you won't know what's out there until you go. Steve Dunn, a fabulous art director from London, put it this way: "One thing I recommend is at some point you should turn everything on its head. Logos usually go lower right, so put them top left. Product shots are usually small, make them big. Instead of headlines being more prominent than the body copy, do the opposite. It's perverse, but I'm constantly surprised how many times it works."11 Don't be different just to be different. You must have a reason to "zag," one beyond just the desire to be different. Bill Bernbach said it best: Be provocative. But be sure your provocativeness stems from your product. You are not right if in your ad you stand a man on his head just to get attention. You are right if [it's done to] show how your product keeps things from falling out of his pockets. Merely to let your imagination run riot, to dream unrelated dreams, to indulge in graphic acrobatics is not being creative. The creative person has harnessed his imagination. He has disciplined it so that every thought, every idea, every word he puts down, every line he draws . . . makes more vivid, more believable, more persuasive the . . . product advantage.12 Consider the opposite of your product. What doesn't the product do? Who doesn't need the product? When is the product a waste of money? Study the inverse problem and see where negative thinking leads. I saw a great opposite idea in a student book. It was a small poster for a paint manufacturer that painters could put up after their job was finished. Above the company's logo, this warning: "Dry Paint." Recently, I saw another good one in the New York Times Magazine. It's called reverse graffiti. If you wipe or sand the grime off the wall of derelict property, words and images can be formed by the cleaned area. The kid described in the article was accused by the local city council of breaking the law."For what?" he asked. "Cleaning without a permit?

Avoid the formula of saying one thing and showing another. "Your kids deserve a licking this summer" . . . and then you have a picture of some kids with lollipops. Get it? Again, this isn't a rule. But if you use this sort of setup, make sure the difference between word and picture is breathtaking. The polarity between the two should fairly crackle. This ad from LeagasDelaney in London is a good example (Figure 3.15). Move back and forth between wide-open, blue-sky thinking and critical analysis. It's like this: Up there in my brain, there's this poet guy. Smokes a lot. Wears black. He's so creative. And "chicks dig 'im." He's got a million ideas. But 999,000 of them suck. He knows this because there's also a certified public accountant up there who tells him so. "That won't work. You suck." The CPA is a no-nonsense guy who clips coupons and knows how to fix the car when the poet runs it into the ditch on his way to Beret World. Between the two of them, though, I manage to come up with a few ideas that actually work. The trick is to give each one his say. Let the poet go first. Be loose. Be wild. Then let the CPA come in, take measurements, and see what actually works. I sense that I'm about to run this metaphor into the ground, so I'll just bow out here by saying, go back and forth between wild dorm-room creativity and critical dad'sbasement analysis, always keeping your strategy statement in mind. See if you can avoid doing the old "exaggeration" thing. Sometimes I think there's this tired old computer program inside every copywriter's and art director's head. I call this programming circuitry the Exaggeration chip. Say you're doing an ad for, oh, a water heater. The Exaggeration chip's first 100 ideas will be knee-jerk scenarios about how cold the water will be if you don't buy this water heater: "Water heater? Easy. What you do is, like, you have ice cubes comin' out of the water faucet. See? 'Cause it's so cold the water faucet will have like ice cubes, see? Ice cubes . . . 'cause they're cold." Now, granted, there are plenty of great commercials out there that A Clean Sheet of Paper 59 Figure 3.15 A very good example of picture playing off word, done by two very naughty British boys. 15934_Sullivan_c03_3p.r.qxp 1/2/08 10:06 AM Page 59 use exaggeration to great effect. I'll just warn you that the E-chip is typically the first mental program many creatives will apply to a problem. Buy a lottery ticket and you'll be so rich that ___________________. (Fill in with I'm-really-rich joke here.) Buy this car and you'll go so fast that ______________________________. (Insert acceleration/cop-giving-ticket joke.) It's just a little too easy. But here's the other thing. The E-chip will rarely lead you to a totally unexpected solution.You will end up somewhere in the same neighborhood as you started, maybe a little further out to the edge, but still nearby. A place you will likely share with everybody else who's working on the problem with an E-chip. In which case, it'll simply come down to who has the wackiest exaggeration. Interpret the problem using different mental processes. See what happens. From a book called Conceptual Blockbusting, by James Adams, I excerpt this list:14 build up dissect transpose eliminate symbolize unify work forward simulate distort work backward manipulate rotate associate transform flatten generalize adapt squeeze compare substitute stretch focus combine abstract purge separate translate verbalize vary expand visualize repeat reduce hypothesize multiply understate define invert exaggerate Put on different thinking caps. How would the folks at today's top agencies solve your problem? Chiat/Day, for instance. How would they solve it at Crispin? At 60 "Hey, Whipple, Squeeze This" 15934_Sullivan_c03_3p.r.qxp 1/2/ 08 10:06 AM Page 60 Goodby? How would they approach your problem at Disney? At Apple? At Amblin? Shake the Etch A Sketch in your head, start over constantly, and come at the problem from wildly different angles. Don't keep sniffing all four sides of the same fire hydrant. Run through the entire neighborhood. Metaphors must've been invented for advertising. They aren't always right for the job, but when they are, they can be a quick and powerful way to communicate. Shakespeare did it: "Shall I compare thee to a summer's day?" In my opinion (and the neo-Freudian Carl Jung's), the mind works and moves through and thinks in and dreams in symbols. Red means ANGER. A dog means LOYAL. A hand coming out of water means HELP. Ad people might say that each of these images has "equity," something they mean by dint of the associations people have ascribed to them over the years.You may be able to use this equity to your client's advantage, particularly when their product or service is intangible like, say, insurance.A metaphor can help make it real. What makes metaphors particularly useful to your craft is they're a sort of conceptual shorthand and say with one image what you might otherwise need 20 words to say. They get a lot of work done quickly and simply. The trick is doing it well. Just picking up an image/symbol and plopping it down next to your client's logo won't work. But when you can take an established image, put some spin on it, and use it in some new and unexpected way that relates to your product advantage, things can get pretty cool. As soon as I put those words on paper,I remembered the marvelous British campaign for the Economist. In the one reprinted here (Figure 3.16), an unadorned keyhole is simply plopped down next to the logo. One stroke is all it takes to give the impression that this business magazine has inside information on corporations. So much for rules. Still, I stand by the advice. Symbols lifted right off the rack usually won't fit your communication needs and typically need some spin put on them.

"Wit invites participation." Part of what makes metaphors in ads so effective is that they involve the reader. They use images already in the reader's mind, twist them to the message's purpose, and ask the reader to close the loop for us. There are other ways you can leave some of the work to the reader, and when you do it correctly, you usually have a better ad. Here's an example. Nikon cameras ran an ad with the headline: "If you can picture it in your head, it was probably taken with a Nikon." Above this headline were four solid black squares, and inside each square was a small headline in white type describing a famous photograph. "A three-year-old boy saluting at his father's funeral." "A lone student standing in front of four tanks." "An American President lifting his pet beagle up by the ears." "A woman crying over the body of a student shot by the National Guard." Instead of showing these famous photos, the negatives are developed in the reader's head. The reader sees JFK Jr. He sees Tiananmen Square. He sees LBJ and Kent State. "Hey, I know all these photos." The reader connects the dots and in doing so is rewarded for applying his intelligence, rewarded for staying with the ad. The client is rewarded, too, with a reader actively closing the loop between the famous photos and the cameras that took them. In a great book called A Smile in the Mind: Witty Thinking in Graphic Design, authors McAlhone and Stuart say that "wit invites participation." When wit is involved, the designer never travels 100% of the way [towards the audience.] . . . The audience may need to travel only 5% or as much as

40% towards the designer in order to unlock the puzzle and get the idea . . . it asks the reader to take part in the communication of the idea. It is as if the designer throws a ball which then has to be caught. So the recipient is alert, with an active mind and a brain in gear.15 Their point about traveling "only 5% or as much as 40%" is an important one. If you leave too much out, you'll mystify your audience. If you put too much in, you'll bore them.

Testing the borders of this sublime area will be where you spend much of your time when you're coming up with ads. Somewhere between showing a picture of a flaming zebra on a unicycle and an ad that reads "Sale ends Saturday" is where you want to be. The wisdom of knock-knock jokes. Consider these one-liners from stand-up comedian Steven Wright: "If a cow laughed, would milk come out her nose? . . . When you open a new bag of cotton balls, are you supposed to throw the top one away? . . . When your pet bird sees you reading the newspaper, does he wonder why you're just sitting there staring at carpeting?" Well, I think it's funny. In the last bit, for instance, the word newspaper begins as reading material and ends as cage-bottom covering. A shift has happened and everything is slightly off. I don't know why these shifts and the sudden introduction of incongruous data make our computers spasm; they just do. You may find that jumping from one point of view to another to introduce a sudden new interpretation is an effective way to add tension and release to the architecture of an ad.That very tension involves the viewer more than a simple expository statement of the same facts. Creative theorist Arthur Koestler noted that a person, on hearing a joke, is "compelled to repeat to some extent the process of inventing the joke, to recreate it in his imagination." Authors McAlhone and Stuart add, "An idea that happens in the mind, stays in the mind . . . it leaves a stronger trace. People can remember that flash moment, the click, and recreate the pleasure just by thinking about it." A good example is this famous poster for VW from the United Kingdom (Figure 3.19).As a viewer, you don't need it spelled out; in your head you quickly put together what happened, backward. "And that, dear students," said the professor of Humor 101, "is why the chicken crossed the road." Suddenly, that's how this section on humor feels to me. Pedantic. So I'll just close by saying that jokes make us laugh by introducing the unexpected. An ad can work the same way. Don't set out to be funny. Set out to be interesting. Funny is a subset of interesting. Funny isn't a language. Funny is an accent. And funny may not even be the right accent. I find it interesting that the Clios, a highly overrated awards show with far too many categories, had a category called "Best Use of Humor." And, curiously, no "Best Use of Seriousness." Funny, serious, heartfelt—none of it matters if you aren't interesting first. Howard Gossage, a famous ad person from the 1950s, said, "People read what interests them, and sometimes it's an ad." Try not to look like an ad. People don't buy magazines to look at ads. So why look like one? This doesn't mean you should make it look like nonsense. Just try not to look like an ad. An ad says, "Turn the page." Perhaps you don't need to stick a logo in the lower right-hand corner. Can you find another way to sign off? Can your TV spot look like documentary footage? Or a soap opera? Try not to sound like an ad. Don't let your concept get in the way of the product. Bernbach said, "Our job is to sell our clients' merchandise . . . not ourselves. To kill the cleverness that makes us shine instead of the product." This can happen, and when clients kill an ad for this reason they may be right. From more than one client, I've heard this dreaded phrase: "Your concept is a 'Visual Vampire.' " What they mean is the concept's execution is so busy it sucks the life out of their commercial message. Be ready for this one. Sometimes clients use the phrase as a bludgeon to kill something unusual they don't like. But sometimes, a few of them are right.* This usually happens when the product bores you. Which means you haven't dug deep enough to find the thing about it that's exciting or interesting. You settle for doing some sort of conceptual gymnastics up front and tacking your boring old product on the back side, hoping the interest from the opening will somehow bleed over to your sales message. But the interesting part of an ad shouldn't be a device that points to the sales message, it should be the sales message. To understand what it means to make your whole ad or commercial be the sales message, consider the analogy of giving your dog a pill. Dogs hate pills, right? So what do you do? You wrap the pill in a piece of baloney. Well, same thing with your commercial's message. Customers hate sales pitches. So you wrap your pitch in an interesting bit, and they're more likely to bite. Unfortunately, most students take this to mean, "Oh, I see. All I have to do is show something interesting and funny for the first 25 seconds and then cut to the product." The answer is no. Because the customer will eat up the 25 seconds of interesting baloney and then walk away, leaving the pill in the dog dish. You gotta wrap that baby right into the middle of the baloney. The two have to be one. Your interesting device cannot just point to the sales message; it must be the sales message. Remember Bernbach's advice: "The product, the product, the product. Stay with the product." Don't get tangled up in unrelated ideas, however fanciful. David Ogilvy used a classical reference to make this same point: "When Aeschines spoke, they said, 'How well he speaks.' But when Demosthenes spoke, they said, 'Let us march against Philip.'" SIMPLE = GOOD, PART II. If you take away one thing from this book, let it be this advice: Simple is almost always better. Maurice Saatchi, of London's M&C Saatchi, on simplicity: "Simplicity is all. Simple logic, simple arguments, simple visual images. If you can't reduce your argument to a few crisp words and phrases, there's something wrong with your argument." "Simplicity, simplicity, simplicity!" Henry David Thoreau, sitting in his shack by the famous pond, penned this oft-quoted line. Seems to me Hank needs a dose of his own medicine: "Simplicity,simplicity,simplicity!" There. That's better. Well, do the same with your ads. Look at this simple Nike piece (Figure 3.20). Every extraneous thing has been shaved away. That reminds me. There's an old axiom called Occam's razor: When you have two correct answers that both solve the problem, the more correct answer is the simplest one. Because it solves the problem with fewer moving parts. It solves the problem more elegantly Simple is hard to miss. I've always thought a stop sign is a perfect metaphor for a good ad. It makes me stop. It is relevant. It has one word. And most of all, it is simple. It says, "STOP." There is no introduction to "stop." No asterisks are needed to understand "stop." And "stop" needs no snappy wrap-up. So how is a stop sign different from a good ad in a magazine? I'm turning the pages and suddenly right in my face is a big, simple, relevant message. How can I ignore it? This Japanese ad touting the safety of Volvo cars stopped me Simple is bigger. On May 7, 1915, a German U-boat sank a passenger ship, the Lusitania, killing some 1,190 civilians, many of them women and children. America was finally too angry to stay out of the Great War, and enlistment posters began to appear in shop windows, one of which is reprinted here . Most other World War I posters were not as visual and instead used headlines like "Irishmen, Avenge the Lusitania!" and "Take Up the Sword of Justice." Seems to me, all these decades later, Simple breaks through advertising clutter. As we noted earlier, the only effective antidote to clutter is simplicity. How can anything else but simplicity break out of clutter? Even the Super Bowl, with its annual collection of eye-popping TV commercials, has its own brand of clutter. Call it "pretty good clutter" if you will. But it's clutter just the same, and you have to find a way to improve what a scientist might call its "signal-to-noise ratio." You have to break out. You can do that only with an idea of sparkling simplicity. The One Show recently honored a commercial created overseas that was sparkling in its simplicity, and inexpensive as well. The camera opens on a woman in a small, dingy room seen from behind glass. She's wearing orange overalls and is tired and dirty— probably a prisoner just getting off work detail. Appearing on the 72 "Hey, Whipple, Squeeze This" Figure 3.23 Google links to billions of sites— all from this simple home page. 15934_Sullivan_c03_3p.r.qxp 1/2/08 10:06 AM Page 72 other side of the glass is her daughter, who asks, "When are you going to get out of here?" The exhausted mother shakes her head dispiritedly; all she can say for sure is, "In a while." Their hands come to the glass in between and touch tenderly. "I love you, Momma," says the girl before leaving. Mother replies, "I love you, too." The camera pulls back and we see the glass is just a shower door and that Mom is in the middle of a long, dirty job of cleaning the tiles in their family shower.The voice-over comes in to conclude this simple tableau with: "Spend less time cleaning. Vim Cream. Cleans the tough stuff. Easily." Keep paring away until you have the essence of your ad. Let's start with three observations from three different men: one dead, one British, and one crazy. Robert Louis Stevenson said, "The only art is to omit." Tony Cox, a fabulous British writer: "Inside every fat ad there's a thinner and better one trying to get out." And then there's Neil French, one of my heroes and an absolutely stellar writer from Singapore. I was lucky enough to meet him onc day, and he walked me through a wonderful exercise in in the art of omitting, of reductionism. He started by drawing a thumbnail sketch of a typical ad (number one in You have your headline, your visual, some body copy, a tagline, and a logo. Okay, he asked, can we make this ad work without the body copy? Maybe we could do that by making the headline work a little harder. We can? Good, let's take out the body copy. That leaves the slightly cleaner layout of number two. What about that tagline? Is it bringing any new information to the ad? No? Then let's broom it. Look, the third layout's even better. Now, about that headline. Is it doing something the visual can't do? And that logo—isn't there some way we can incorporate it into the visual? Ultimately, Neil reduced his ad to one thing. He suggested I do the same with my next ad. Get it down to one thing. Sometimes it's just a headline. Sometimes a picture. Either way, he said, the math always works out the same. Every element you add to a layout reduces the importance of all the other elements. And conversely, every item you subtract raises the visibility and importance of what's left. I admit, this kind of draconian reductionism is hard to pull off, especially when you have a client wanting to put more in an ad, not less. In my career I've done it only once. But to this day, that ad remains one of my favorites. It's the one you see here, reminding store buyers to stock Lee jeans . No logo. No headline. The less you have to put in the ad, the better. The writer Saki said, "When baiting a trap with cheese, always leave room for the mouse."

LET'S START WITH OUTDOOR. Billboards force you to be simple. In all of advertising, billboards are the best place to practice the art of simplicity. In fact, my first mentor,Tom McElligott, told me if you have outdoor in the media mix for the campaign you're about to do, start there first. Nothing focuses you on a problem like this medium. It's been said that a board should have no more than seven words. Any more and a passing driver can't read it. But then you add the client's logo. One or two words. Now you're up to nine. And if your visual is something that takes one or two beats to understand, well, in my opinion, you've already got too much on your plate.

Outdoor is a great place to get outrageous. Big as they are on the landscape, outdoor boards are an event, not just an ad. In fact, what makes for a good print advertisement doesn't necessarily make for a good billboard. Whatever you do, don't create something just okay. The final size of a billboard out there in the world only magnifies how an idea is just OKAY. You don't wanna be just okay. Check this board out; it's way better than okay. Adidas brought to life its "Impossible is nothing" tagline with a live-action board in New Zealand.To launch the Fifa World Cup games there, the agency (TBWA/Whybin) created a reverse bungee "Sky Screamer" ride that looked like a giant soccerball, setting it up in front of a large image of a popular player, Steven Gerrard. Fans who purchased a ball were given the chance to "Be the Ball" and were strapped in on seats inside. A sportscaster gave commentary on a match and at the exact second they described Gerrard kicking the ball, the Sky Screamer launched, reaching 105 mph in two seconds (Figure . Outdoor begs for the ostentatious. Go for broke. Remember, you're in "made-you-look, made-you-look" territory here. Outdoor companies, prop makers, and tech firms can help bring just about any wild idea to life. And now with the confluence of the Web and mobile phones, people on the street can interact with boards, sending either video or text for all the world to see.

Your outdoor must delight people. Except for the handful of great ideas in the One Show every year, most of the outdoor I see really sucks. When an ad in a magazine isn't good, I can turn the page. But if I live across the street from a bad billboard, there's nothing I can do about it except close my curtains. Copywriter Howard Gossage didn't believe outdoor boards were a true advertising medium: "An advertising medium is a medium that incidentally carries advertising but whose primary function is to provide something else: entertainment, news, etc....Your exposure to television commercials is conditional on their being accompanied by entertainment that is not otherwise available. No such parity or tit-for-tat or fair exchange exists in outdoor advertising. . . . I'm afraid the poor old billboard doesn't qualify as a medium at all; its medium, if any, is the scenery around it and that is not its to give away."16 The city of Sao Paulo, Brazil, has already outlawed billboards, and here in America several states are weighing similar bans. Well, until the day billboards are outlawed altogether (either as "corporate littering" or perhaps "retinal trespassing"), you owe the citizens of the town where your outdoor appears—you owe them your very best work. You must delight them.

Learn to recognize big ideas when you have them. There will come a time when you see a great idea in a One Show annual, a campaign that'll make you go, "Damn! I thought of that once!" It's a hard thing to see, "your" idea done, and done well. That's why you have to be smart enough to pursue a promising idea once you've stumbled onto it. I'm reminded of a line by Ralph Waldo Emerson: "In every work of genius we recognize our own rejected thoughts." See that one idea you have up on the wall? The one that's so much better than the others? Investigate why. There may be oil under that small patch of land. A big idea is almost always incredibly simple. So simple, you wonder why nobody's thought of it before. It has "legs" and can work in a lot of different executions in all kinds of media. Coming up with a big idea is one skill. Recognizing a big idea is another skill. Develop both. Big ideas transcend strategy. When you finally come upon a big idea, you may look up from your pad to discover that you've wandered off strategy. That's okay. The gold isn't always in them hills. But gold is gold, and good account people will understand this and help you retool the strategy to get the client past this unexpected turn in the road. My friend Mike Lescarbeau compares a big idea to a nuclear bomb. Does it really have to land precisely on target to work? Don't keep runnin' after you catch the bus. After you've covered the walls with ideas and you've identified some concepts you really like, stop.And I mean covered the walls.This isn't permission to stop because you're tired or you have a few things that aren't half-bad. It's a reminder to keep one eye on the deadline. Blue-skying is great. You have to do it. But there comes a time (and you'll get better at recognizing it) when you'll have to cut bait and start working on the really good ones. You have a fixed amount of time, so you'll need to devote some of it to making what's good great.

CHAPTER EIGHT

Write When You Get Work

BEFORE WE BEGIN, A QUICK NOTE. The first edition of this book came out in 1998—last century, basically. At the time, the possibilities of advertising online were just starting to be realized, and since then the number of other media used to deliver advertising has gone kaleidoscopic. That said, to begin our discussion of advertising ideas we still have to start somewhere. And for the purposes of this book, we'll make the humble print ad our starting point. No, it's not interactive and it doesn't link to other print ads.You don't have to go to L.A. to make a print ad, and it usually ends life under a puppy or a bird. But in its simple two dimensions and blank white space, it contains all the challenges we need in order to discuss the creative process. So let's begin. Come up with a lot of ideas. Cover the wall. It's tempting to think that the best advertising people just peel off great campaigns 10 minutes before they're due. But that is perception, not reality. 15934_Sullivan_c04_3p.r.qxp 1/2/08 10:07 AM Page 81 In fact, "Perception/Reality" (the famous Rolling Stone campaign) is a perfect case in point. Those great ads that you may have seen in all the awards annuals are only the tip of the iceberg. The rest of it, a four-foot-high pile of other layouts, sat in writer Bill Miller's office for years. So massive was the pile of ideas that what he didn't use as ads actually served as a small table. As a creative person, you will discover your brain has a built-in tendency to want to reach closure, even rush to it. Evolution has left us with circuitry that doesn't like ambiguity or unsolved problems. Its pattern-recognition wiring evolved for keeping us out of the jaws of lions, tigers, and bears—not for making lateral jumps to discover unexpected solutions. But in order to get to a great idea, which is usually about the 500th one to come along, you'll need to resist the temptation to give in to the anxiety and sign off on the first passable idea that shows up. Linus Pauling: "The best way to get a good idea is to get a lot of ideas. . . . At first, ideas seem as hard to find as crumbs on an oriental rug. Then they start coming in bunches. When they do, don't stop to analyze them; if you do you'll stop the flow, the rhythm, the magic. Write them down and go on to the next one." Which leads to our next point. Quick sketches of your ideas are all you need during the creative process. Don't curb your creativity by stopping the car and getting out every time you have an idea you want to work out. Just put the concept on paper and continue moving forward. You'll cover more ground this way. Tack the best ideas on the wall. Seeing them up there all in a bunch helps you determine whether there are campaigns forming and where there are holes that need to be filled. You keep working on the details on your pad. But up there on the wall the big picture begins to take shape. Write. Don't talk. Write. Don't talk about the concepts you're working on. Talking turns energy you could use to be creative into talking about being creative. 82 "Hey, Whipple, Squeeze This" 15934_Sullivan_c04_3p.r.qxp 1/2/08 10:07 AM Page 82 It's also likely to send your poor listener looking for the nearest espresso machine because an idea talked about is never as exciting as the idea itself. If you don't believe me, call me up sometime and I'll describe the movie The Matrix to you. There's an old saying: "A manuscript, like a fetus, is never improved by showing it to somebody before it is completed." Work. Just work.The time will come to unveil. For now, just work.The best ad people I know are the silent-but-deadly kind. You never hear them out in the hallways talking about their ideas. They're working. Write hot. Edit cold. Get it on paper, fast and furious. Be hot. Let it pour out. Don't edit anything when you're coming up with the ads. Then, later, be ruthless. Cut everything that is not A-plus work. Put all the A-minus and B-plus stuff off in another pile you'll revisit later. Everything that's B-minus on down, put on the shelf for emergencies. The wastepaper basket is the writer's best friend. —Novelist Isaac Singer Once you get on a streak, ride it. When the words finally start coming, stay on it. Don't break for lunch. Don't put it off till Monday. You'd be surprised how cold some trails get once you leave them for a few minutes. Athletes call this place (where everything is working, where all the pistons are firing) "the Zone." Some artists call it "the White Moment." I call it "that Brief Moment each week when I Don't Suck." The moral: Never walk away from a hot keyboard (or a drawing pad). If it makes you laugh out loud, make it work. Somehow. You know those really funny ideas you get that make you laugh and say, "Wouldn't it be great if we could really do that?" Those are often the very best ideas, and it is only your superego/parent/ internalized client saying you can't do it.

You've stumbled on a mischievous idea. Something you shouldn't do. That's a good sign you're on to something you should do. Revisit it.

HOW TO WRITE HEADLINES BETTER THAN THIS ONE. Get puns out of your system right away. Puns, in addition to being the lowest thing on the joke food chain, have no persuasive value. It's okay to think them. It's okay to write them down. Just make sure you toss them. Don't just start writing headlines willy-nilly. Break it down. Do willy first.Then move on to nilly. If you have an assignment that calls for a more verbal solution, don't just start spitting out the headlines. Instead, methodically explore different attributes and benefits of your product as you write. Here's an example from my files. The project is a bourbon. The client can afford only a small-space newspaper campaign and a billboard or two. They've said they want to see their bottle, so the finished ads will likely be just a bottle and a headline. After some discussion with the account folks about tone ("thoughtful, intellectual"), the art director and I consider several avenues for exploration. The bourbon's age might be one way to go. Bourbon, by law, is aged a minimum of two years, often up to eight, sometimes longer. So we start there to see what happens. We put our feet up and immediately begin discussing the movie The Terminator. Sometime after lunch we take a crack at the "aging" thing. AGE IDEAS Order a drink that takes nine years to get. Like to hear how it's made? Do you have nine years? (Note: On the pages from the actual file, there are about five false starts for each one of these headlines. Tons of scratch-outs and halfwitted ideas that go nowhere.) Nine years inside an oak barrel in an ugly warehouse. Our idea of quality time. After nine years of trickle-down economics, it's ready just in time. Nine long years in a barrel. One glorious hour in a glass. Okay, nine years. What else happens in nine years? What about the feeling of the slow passage of time?

Continental drift happens faster than this bourbon. Mother Nature made it whiskey. Father Time made it bourbon. We can't make it slow enough. What wind does to mountains, time does to this bourbon. On May 15th, we"ll be rotating Barrel #1394 one-quarter turn to the left. Just thought you'd like to know. Tree rings multiply. Glaciers speed by. And still the bourbon waits. Maybe one of these might work. There's another take on age we might try—namely, how long the label's been on the market. Not the age of the whiskey, but of the brand. HISTORY OF BRAND IDEAS First bottled when other bourbons were knee-high to a swizzle stick. First bottled back when American History was an easy course. First bottled when American History was called Current Events. First bottled when the Wild West meant

Kentucky. Smoother than those young whippersnapper bourbons. Back in 1796, this bourbon was the best available form of central heating. The recipe for this bourbon has survived since 1796. Please don't bury it in a mint julep. Write us for free information on what you can do with wine coolers. We've been making it continuously since 1796. (Not counting that brief unpleasantness in the 1920s.) If you can't remember the name, just ask for the bourbon first bottled when Chester A. Arthur was president. 110 years old and still in the bars every night. If we could get any further behind the times, we would. Are we behind the tymes? A blast from the past. First bottled before billboards. This premium bourbon was first marketed via ox. Introduced 50 years before ice cubes.

Okay, maybe there's some stuff we could use from that list. Maybe not. So far we've played with aging and brand history. What about where it's made? KENTUCKY IDEAS Kind of like great Canadian whiskey. Only it's bourbon. And from Kentucky. Kind of like an old Kentucky mule. Classic, stubborn, and plenty of kick. From the third floor of an old warehouse in Kentucky, heaven. Warming trend expected out of Kentucky. Now available to city folk. If this ad had a jingle, it'd be "Dueling Banjos." What the Clampetts would serve the Trumps. This bourbon is the real McCoy. Even the Hatfields agreed. It's not just named after a creek in Kentucky. It's made from it. This is a beautiful picture of a tiny creek that flows through the back hills of Kentucky. (Picture of bottle.) Old as the hills it's from. Smooth. Deep. Hard to find. Kind of like the creek we get the water from. Hand-bottled straight from a barrel in Kentucky. Strap in. Tastes like a Kentucky sunset looks. Its Old Kentucky Home was a barrel. Maybe those last two might also make for good outdoor, given how short they are. We make a note. Remember, the point here isn't, hey, let's see how many headlines can we write, but rather how many different doors can we go through? How many different ways can we look at the same problem? Okay, now let's see what can be done with the way some people drink bourbon—straight. Or perhaps the time of day it's drunk. (Wait a minute. Bad word.) HOW-YOU-DRINK-IT IDEAS With a bourbon this good, you don't need to show breasts in the ice cubes. In fact, you don't need ice cubes. Neither good bourbons nor bad arguments hold water.

Water ruins baseball games and bourbon. For a quiet night, try it without all the noisy ice. Great after the kids are in bed. Perfect after they're in college. Mixes superbly with a rocking chair and a dog. You don't need water to enjoy this premium bourbon. A fire might be nice. Perfect for those quiet times. Like between marriages. As you can see, each one of these doors we went through—age, history, Kentucky—led to another hallway, full of other doors to try. Which is one of the marvelous things about writing. It's not simply a way of getting things down on paper. Writing is a way of thinking— thinking with your pencil, your wrist, and your spine and just seeing where a thing goes. Clearly, a few of the bourbon ideas presented here aren't very good. (Lord knows, you may think they all suck.) But like Pickett's Charge at Gettysburg, with 15,000 soldiers, one or two are going to make it over the wall. One more little case study, this one for one of the nation's largest airlines. They had just purchased a whole bunch of new 777s and A320s (read: "roomier wide-body jets"), and they wanted print ads to promote the benefits to business travelers. Well, if we break it down, perhaps some of the concepts could focus on more personal space and some on the comfort of the seat itself. We could further break it down into ideas that are headline driven and ideas that are visually driven. PERSONAL-SPACE IDEAS, HEADLINE DRIVEN Maybe we could try some headlines that would work by themselves (or perhaps with a "flat" visual like a shot of a wide aisle or a roomy seat). Most passengers would give their right arm for more room for their right arm. Everyone who'd like more personal space, raise your hand, if possible. () Getting incredibly close to people is fine for encounter groups, not planes. Now even luggage has more elbow room.

You can use a camera lens to make your planes look big. Or you can buy big planes. Wouldn't it be great if an airline advertised wider planes instead of wider smiles? Choose one: Bigger bags of peanuts. Bigger smiles. Bigger planes. We thought so. Airline math:The wider the plane, the shorter the flight feels. PERSONAL-SPACE IDEAS, A LITTLE MORE VISUALLY DRIVEN This, only higher. (VISUAL: A well-worn La-Z-Boy recliner.) There are two places you can stretch out and let someone solve your problems. With ours, you get miles. (VISUAL: Shrink's office.) Which one would you take on a long trip? Exactly. Now let's move on to planes. (VISUAL: Small car versus big SUV.) We put it in our planes. (VISUAL: Man in his living room, football game on TV, quizzically looking at flattened area of shag rug where his La-Z-Boy recliner used to be.) Traveling has always been easier when you have room to yourself. (VISUAL: Old family photo of three kids fussing at each other in the backseat of station wagon.) Da Vinci never designed a plane that worked, but he had this cool idea about personal space. (VISUAL: Da Vinci drawings of the body showing the arc of the arms, motion of legs.) EMOTIONAL BENEFITS, A LITTLE MORE VISUALLY-

DRIVEN What would happen if we concentrated more on the emotional benefits of a wider more comfortable seat? If our new seat doesn't put you to sleep, try reading the whole ad. (VISUAL: Airline seat with long copy and lots of callouts.) It doesn't matter how roomy a seat is if you don't like the service. (VISUAL: Little boy dwarfed in a big dentist's chair.) Almost every passenger arrives feeling human. (VISUAL: Dog getting out of airline pet carrier.)

"Some settling may occur during shipment." (VISUAL: Seat shot with sleeping passenger.) With our new seats, you won't have to count for long. (VISUAL: A single sheep with caption under it:"One.") () When you fly with us, never promise "I'll work on the plane." (VISUAL: Close-up shot of computer screen with menu button of "Sleep" backlit.) () Have you always done your best thinking way up high somewhere? (VISUAL: A kid's treehouse seen from way at bottom of ladder, two sneakered feet sticking out of the door.) After I've finished writing a list about this long, I'll go back over it and make a little mark () next to my favorites. Then I transfer those few ideas over to a clean sheet of paper and start all over. I mean, start all over. Pretend you have nothing so far. The fact is, there are only 22 airline ideas in the preceding list—22. We cannot seriously believe we'll have crafted a ticket-selling, brand-building, One Show–winning ad after 22 stinking tries. We'll need hundreds. If that sounds daunting, get ready for a long and hard career. This is the way it's done. Remember, the wastepaper basket is the writer's best friend. If the ad needs a headline, write 100. Sorry, but there's no shortcut. Write 100 of them. And don't confuse this with Tom Monahan's exercise of 100-Mile-an-Hour Thinking.1 (That's a pretty good exercise, too, but better for the very beginning of the creative process. In that exercise,Tom advises creative people to turn on the fire hydrant for 20 minutes and catch every single first thought that comes out. Each idea goes on a separate Post-it Note, with absolutely no editing.) Nope, here I'm not talkin' about 100-mile-per-hour writing. This is sitting down and slowly cranking out 100 workable lines—100 lines that range from decent, to heynot-bad, to whoa-that-rocks. The key is they all have to be pretty good. To prove this very point, Sally Hogshead bravely posted all of the BMW motorcycle headlines she came up with to get to her final five ads featured in the One Show and Communication Arts Read the list and you'll see a copywriter really thinking it through, rattling different doorknobs up and down the conceptual hallway, sometimes writing about the union of rider and bike, sometimes about goose bumps. They're all pretty darn good. (She's good at other stuff, too—particularly career advice for creatives. Check out her web site at sallyhogshead.com.) Even atheists kneel on a BMW. • Some burn candles when praying. Others, rubber. • There are basilicas, cathedrals, mosques. And then there''s Route 66. • Buy one before the Church bans such marriages. • People take vows of chastity to feel this way. • More Westminster Abbey than Cal Tech. • Runners get a high from jogging around a track at 8 miles per hour. Pathetic. • This is exactly the sort of intimacy that would frighten Jesse Helms. • Fits like a glove. A metallic silver, fuelinjected, 150-horsepower glove. • You don't get off a BMW so much as take it off. • Relationships this intimate are illegal in some states. • Usually, this kind of connection requires surgery. • Didn't George Orwell predict man and machine would eventually become one? • The Church has yet to comment on such a marriage of man and machine. • Somebody call Ray Bradbury. We've combined man and machine. • Do you become more machine, or does it become more human? • And then there were two. • "Oh look, honey. What a sweet looking couple." • If you ever connect like this with a person, marry them. • Fits tighter than OJ's glove./• Why some men won't stop and ask directions. • "Darling, is that...a smudge of motor oil on your collar?" •

The road is calling. Don't get its message by voicemail. • The feeling is more permanent than any tattoo. • "Yippee! I'm off to my root canal!" • Your inner child is fluent in German. • The last day of school, any day of the year. • Your heart races, your senses tingle. Then you turn it on. • There is no known antidote once it gets into your blood. • There are no words to describe it. Unless "Wooohoo!" counts. • No amusement park ride can give this feeling. • If he had a mood ring on, it'd be bright green. • Never has a raccoon baking in the sun smelled sweeter. • How "joie de vivre" translates into German. • Put as much distance as possible between you and the strip mall. • Off, off, off, off-road. • If it had a rearview mirror, you'd see your troubles in it. • There's something worth racing towards at the end of this road: another 25 miles. • The best psychotherapy doesn't happen lying on a couch. • A remote control is a more dangerous machine. • A carnivore in the food chain of bikes. • If you're trying to find yourself, you sure as hell won't find it on the sofa. • If you had eight hours, alone, no radio, imagine what you could think about. • Where is it written the love for your motorcycle must be platonic? • Seems preoccupied. Comes home later than usual. Always wanting to get out of the house. • You possess a motorcycle. You're possessed by a BMW. • Let's see. You're either riding it, or wishing you were riding it, or thinking about the last time you rode it. • Men who own a BMW have something else to think about every 22 seconds. • You've got just one companion on the road. Find one you can get along with. • What you're seeing is his soul. His body's in a meeting in Cincinnati right now. • Merge with traffic. Not every other motorcycle owner. • Your estimated time of arrival just got bumped up. • Where do you drive when you daydream? • And together they rode off into the sunset. • What walking on air actually looks like. • The invitation said to bring your significant other. She thinks it's her. • Lust fueled by gasoline. • The bike, the girlfriend. Guess which model he'll trade in first. • She wonders why she sometimes feels like a third wheel. • Room for luggage. None for baggage. The point here is both quantity and quality. You don't get to great until you do a whole bunch of good. Save the operative part of the headline for the very end. You know that single part of a headline where the concept comes to life? That key word or phrase where the idea is unveiled? Save that unveiling for the end of your headline.

Take, for example, this headline from the preceding list of airline ideas. Almost every passenger arrives feeling human. (VISUAL: Dog getting out of airline pet carrier.) The line could have been constructed other ways: You'll feel human when you arrive, thanks to our new seats. When the seats let you sleep, almost everybody feels human on arrival. Some of the punch is missing, isn't it? It feels better when you save your wrap-up punch for the end of your sentence. It has more surprise and power. Never use fake names in a headline. (Or copy. Or anywhere else for that matter.) "Little Billy's friends at school call him different." Lines like this drive me nuts. "Little Billy will never know his real father." Hey, little Billy, c'mere. Go back and tell your copywriter that a strange man in the park said to tell him he's a hack. Anybody reading this kind of crap knows these ad names are fake. And an irritating kind of fake at that. Like those manufactured relatives they put inside of picture frames at stores. Avoid fake people. Avoid fake names. There are times, however, when using a person's name is the only way the concept will work. And in the hands of a seasoned team, as in this Vitro-Robertson ad for client Taylor guitars , it can be done beautifully. It comes down to style. To how gracefully and believably you pull it off. Don't let the headline flex any muscles when the visual is doing the heavy lifting. As it is in dancing, one should lead, one should follow. If your visual is a hardworking idea, let your headline quietly clean up the work left to it. And if the headline is brilliant, well-crafted, and covers all the bases, the visual (if one exists at all) should be merely icing on the cake. Remember, the rule of thumb is never show what you're saying and never say what you're showing. This ad for Harley-Davidson motorcycles is a perfect example . By itself, the visual is fairly tame. By itself, the headline is dull and almost meaningless. But together, they make one of the best ads I've ever seen. When it's just a headline, it'd better be a pretty good headline. One of the best campaigns of all time (in this writer's opinion) is Abbott Meade Vickers's work for the Economist . This campaign was basically an outdoor campaign of brilliant headlines against a backdrop of the color red (lifted from the magazine's masthead). Several of the finished ads are pictured throughout this book, but the lines all by themselves are also great lessons in brilliant copywriting. I include my favorites here. Think someone under the table. If you're already a reader, ask your chauffeur to hoot as you pass this poster. "Can I phone an Economist reader, please, Chris?" Don't be a vacancy on the board.

If your assistant reads The Economist, don't play too much golf. Retire early with a good read. Look forward to school reunions. It's lonely at the top, but at least there's something to read. Eiq2 If they did brain transplants, would you be a donor or a recipient? In opinion polls, 100% of Economist readers had one. If someone gave you a penny for your thoughts, would they get change? Would you like to sit next to you at dinner? Think outside the dodecahedron. Ever go blank at the crucial . . . thingy? Cures itchy scalps. "Is it me, or is quantum physics easier these days?" Certain headlines are currently checked out.You may use them when they are returned. Lines like "Contrary to popular belief . . ." or "Something is wrong when . . ." are pretty much used up. Get over it. Do something new.

Don't use a model number in the headline. Client numbers like "TX-17" may seem familiar to you. But you're used to it; you work on the account. In a headline, they serve only as a speed bump. They're not words, they're numerals, so they force readers to switch gears in their heads to 17, x45, 13z42 to get through your sentence. SOME NOTES ON DESIGN (FROM A WRITER). Something has to dominate the ad. Whether it's a big headline, a large visual, or a single word floating in white space, somebody's got to be the boss. It's easy to spot ads where the art director (or perhaps client) couldn't decide what was most important.The ads are usually in three big pieces.The visual takes up a third of the page.A headline takes up the next third. And a combination of body copy–logo–tagline brings up the rear. And the whole thing has about as much cohesion as a cookie in the rain.

Your ad needs a boss, as well as an overall visual hierarchy. The late Roy Grace, one of the famous art directors from Doyle Dane Bernbach, spoke to this issue: There has to be a point on every page where the art director and the writer want you to start. Whether that is the center of the page, the top right-hand corner, or the left-hand corner, there has to be an understanding, an agreement, and a logical reason where you want people to look first.2 Avoid trends in execution. Don't take your cues from design trends you see in the awards books. (For one thing, if they're in the books, they're already two years old. The One Show book arrives, literally, on a slow boat from China, where it's printed.) But this is about more than being up-todate. It's about concentrating on the soul of an ad instead of the width of its lapels. Do as you wish, by all means, but I'll warn you of two things. Riding the wave of every passing fad will make your portfolio look trendy and derivative. Also, when you enter your piece in a show, the judges (who've seen just about every trend come and go) will likely deep-six it in a heartbeat. Develop a look no one else has. You've got to find something your client can call their own: a shape, a color, a design, something that is unique. Helmut Krone: "I was working on Avis and looking for a page style. That's very important to me, a page style. I feel that you should be able to tell who's running that ad at a distance of twenty feet."3 What's interesting about Krone's statement is that he's not talking about billboards but print ads. And if you look at his two most famous campaigns, they stand up to the test. You could identify his Volkswagen and Avis ads from across a street The longer I'm in this business, the more I'm convinced art direction is where the major battle for brand building happens. Once you establish a look, once you stake out a design territory, no one else can use it without looking like your brand. The Economist practically owns the color red. IBM continues to letterbox its television with those iconic blue bars. And Apple Computer's signature color of a clean white screams "Apple" before the first word of copy is read. Own something visual. Always do ads with babies or children. Oh, and another thing. Always, always write the headline in the script of a child's handwriting. It's very cute, don't you think? / And don't forget to have at least two of the letters be adorably backward. Backward 's are best. Backward O's don't work. Here's a regular O and here's a backward O. See? Not as adorable as a backward . (Just checking to see if you're awake.) WRITING BODY COPY. Writing well, rule #1: Write well. I don't think people read body copy. I think we've entered a frenzied era of coffee-guzzling, e-mail-sending channel surfers who honk the nanosecond the light turns green and have the attention span of a flashbulb. If the first nine words of body copy aren't "May we send you beer and money for free?," word 10 isn't read. Just my opinion, mind you. Raymond McKinney at The Martin Agency had it right when he wrote a line for those condensed-book study aids: "Cliff Notes. When you don't have time to see the movie." Yet when I write body copy, long or short, I work hard at making it as smart and persuasive and readable as I can. I suggest you do the same. Because a few people are going to read it. And the ones who do, you want. They're interested. They're peering in your shop window. So as much as I hammer away on the importance of visual solutions, when you have to write, write smartly. With passion, intelligence, and honesty. And when you've said what you need to say, stop. Five rules for effective speechwriting from Winston Churchill. 1. Begin strongly. 2. Have one theme

3. Use simple language. 4. Leave a picture in the listener's mind. 5. End dramatically. Write like you talk. In copy for ads, in letters to clients, and in memos to colleagues, write like you talk. For some reason, when handed a pen and asked to write something that will be seen by others, 9 out of 10 people decide an authoritarian tone is somehow more persuasive than clear English. Consider this memo from my files. It was written by a man about whom, were you to meet him, you'd say, "Sharp guy, that Bob. I want him on my account." Yet Bob wrote the following memo. (What he was trying to say was the program was killed because it was too costly.) Effective late last week the Flavor-iffic® project was shelved by the Flavor-Master Consumer Products Division Management. The reasoning had to do with funding generated covering cost of entry, not cost of entry as it would relate to test market in '95, but as it would relate to expansion, if judged successful across major pieces of geography in '96 and beyond. In sum, the way Flavor-Master new products division served up Flavor-iffic® to Consumer Products Division Management was that if Flavor-Master were to relax financial parameters for Flavor-iffic® in '95, '96 and '97, in effect have Corporate fund the program, Consumer Products Division could recommend to Corporate to proceed with the program. The decision was made at the Consumer Products Division Management level that Corporate would most probably not accept that and the subject was taken no further. Except for the name "Flavor-iffic," I swear, every word of this memo is real. The program was killed because it was too costly. That's nine words. Bob, in 143 words, was not only unable to get that nine-word message across, he

effectively lobotomized his audience with a torrent of corporate nonsense that said nothing. It couldn't be decoded. Bob proudly dictated this Rosetta stone, snapped his suspenders, and took the elevator down to the lobby, thinking he'd done his bit to turn the wheels of capitalism for the day.

Yet when he got home, he probably didn't talk that way to his wife. Honey, RE: supper. It has come to my attention, and the concurrent attention of the other family members (i.e., Janice, Bill, and Bob Jr.), that your gravy has inconsistencies of viscosity (popularly known as "lumps"), itself not a disturbing event were it not for the recent disappearance of the family dog. Write like you talk. Write with a smooth, easy rhythm that sounds natural. Obey the rules of grammar and go easy on the adjectives. Short sentences are best. One-word sentences? Fine. End with a preposition if you want to. And if it feels right, begin a sentence with "and." Just be clear. Through it all, remember, you are selling something. Easy to forget when you start slinging words. Write like you would talk if you were the brand. Every brand has a personality. You could describe Apple Computer's personality perhaps as "benevolent intelligence." Read any piece of copy in any Apple ad from the last 10 years—doesn't matter if it's an old ad for an Apple Lisa, or an iMac, or an iPhone. No matter what Apple work you read, you'll feel like you're listening to the same smart big brother, one who wants to sit in the chair with you in front of the keyboard and show you how easy and smart and cool technology can be. Successful brands discover their own distinct voices and then stick with them year after year. If you're inheriting an established voice, you can learn its cadences by reading their previous advertising. If you have a new brand or you're creating a new voice for an old brand, consider yourself lucky. It's one of the most creative and rewarding things you can do in this business—discovering "who" a brand is and giving it shape and form and voice. This isn't done to create stylish writing. What you're doing is creating a brand personality, an important point in a marketplace where the physical differences between products are getting smaller and smaller. Let's say, for example, you're working on a car account. Most of the time, it's likely you'll have to show the car.Your ad may feel half art-directed already, and in a sense it is. So if it comes down to showing just a headline and a picture of a car, your headline ought to have a voice no one else does. Here are three car headlines: If you run out of gas, it's easy to push. We'll never make it big. It's ugly, but it gets you there. Here are three more: In a fuel-obsessed society, is it blasphemy to suggest that a car should be fun to drive? A luxury sedan based on the belief that all of the rich are not idle. The people with money are still spending it, but with infinitely more wisdom. Can you tell which ones are from Volkswagen and which from BMW? It's pretty easy. Which is as it should be. Before you start writing copy, have the basic structure of your argument in mind. Know where you're going to go. "Okay, I've got to come off that headline, then hit A, B, and then end on C." If you neglect this preparation, you will buzz about in a meaningless pattern, like a fly on a summer screen. Don't have what they call a "pre-ramble" in your body copy. The first paragraph of copy in many ads is usually a waste of the reader's time, a repetition of what's already been said in the headline. Consider the analogy of a door-to-door salesman. Your headline is what he says through the crack in the door: his name, what he is selling, and why it's better than the other guy's stuff. Okay, the reader has let you in. And now you're in the foyer. Don't waste time in your first paragraph being reintroductory. "Hi. Remember me? I'm the guy who was out in front of your door two seconds ago. Remember? Said my name, what I'm selling, and why it's better than that other guy's stuff?" Get to the point. It's time for the details. Put your most interesting, surprising, or persuasive point in the first line if you can. You're lucky if people read your headline and luckier yet if they let you into the foyer by reading your copy. Your body copy should reflect the overall concept of the ad. When you start writing, borrow from your concept's imagery, lift colors from its palette. This advice isn't given for stylistic reasons. It helps keep the ad simple. One concept, one voice, one style. Don't overdo this, a common mistake that leaves copy looking amateurish. Use it as you would a spice. In particular, resist the urge to do a "snappy" last line. I suggest ending with the client's address and phone number. "It's not fair to inflict your own style on a strategy." This is from Ed McCabe, one of the great writers of the 1970s. Your job is to present the client's case as memorably as you can, not to come up with another great piece for your portfolio. You want to do both. But you aren't likely to do both if you're concentrating on style. Don't worry about style. It will be expressed no matter what you do. Style is part of the way your brain is wired. Just concentrate on solving the client's problem well. The rest will just happen. Eschew obfuscation. My point exactly. Those words say what I mean to say, but they aren't as clear as they could be. This doesn't mean your writing has to be flat-footed, just understandable. E.B.White said, "Be obscure clearly." Pretend you're writing a letter. Why write to the masses? It's one person reading your ad, isn't it? So write to one person. Write a letter. It's a good voice to use when you're writing copy. It's intimate. It keeps you from lecturing. The best copy feels like a conversation, not a speech. One person talking to another. Not a corporate press release typed in the PR department by some guy named Higgs .

Provide detail. In headlines, in body copy, anywhere you can say something specific and concrete, do it. It will make your argument more persuasive and your ad more interesting. Here's an example of the power of detail. The headline read: "It began 400 years before Christ. It is visible from Mars.You can touch it this spring." Punctuated by a small picture of the Great Wall of China, the details in this headline made me keep reading about Royal Viking's cruises to China. Once you lay your sentences down, spackle between the joints. Use transitions to flow seamlessly from one benefit to the next. Each sentence should come naturally out of the one that precedes it. When you've done it well, you shouldn't be able to take out any sentence without disrupting the flow and structure of the entire piece. (This fragile coherence of beautiful writing is lost on many clients and is one of the reasons copywriters are often seen mumbling to themselves at bus stops.) Break your copy into as many short paragraphs as you can. Short paragraphs are less daunting. I've never read William Faulkner's classic Intruder in the Dust for this very reason. Those eight-page paragraphs look like work to me. Remember, nobody ever had to read People magazine with a bookmark. This isn't an argument for dumbing down your work. Be as smart as you can be. Just don't write paragraphs the size of shower curtains, okay? When you're done writing the copy, read it aloud. I discovered this one the hard way. I had to present some copy to a group of five clients. I read it to them aloud. It was only during the act of reading it this way I discovered how wretched my copy was. school mistakes, seeing the flat reaction of the clients' faces, hearing my voice crack, feeling the flop sweat, it's all coming back to me. When you're done writing, read it aloud. Awkward constructions and wire-thin segues have a way of revealing themselves when read aloud. When you're done writing your body copy, go back and cut it by a third. Proofread your own work. Don't depend on Spell-Check. First of all, that's lazy writing. Second, Spell-Check can't tell the difference between your and you're. (If you have to use any computer program on your writing, If you have to have one, make your tagline an anthem. If you have to craft a tagline, work on it first. Do it early in the process of creating a campaign idea. Try to write about something bigger than just the client's product. Own some high ground. In my opinion, the best ever written was for Nike: "Just Do It." That's not about shoes.

It's not just about sports, either; it's about life. But it sold a lot of shoes. In addition to being cool because it's about more than just some product, an anthem allows you executional freedom later on when you may have to go in new tactical directions and still work off the same campaign. But do you really have to have a tagline? A slogan? It's just one more thing to cram in an ad. One more element to clamor for attention. From what I've seen, few taglines bring any new information to an ad. They're usually piffle. "Looking Backward, but Poised Toward the Future . . .Today." "A Century of Excellence for Over 50 Years." Should your client insist on a tagline, I refer you to this pifflegeneration device John Lyons included in his book Guts. "Simply pick one word from each column," he wrote, "string them together, and you've created a terrific corporate slogan.

"Commitment to an Understanding of Excellence." "The Spirit of Winning through Quality." Ultimately, they're all the same. In my opinion, unless you've penned a "Just Do It," just don't. I once saw a tagline tragically misfire, injuring several. The line was for Stouffer's frozen entrées. The way Stouffer's wanted you to read it was: "People Expect Us to Be Better." But if you read "People Expect Us to Be Better," it left a bad taste in your mouth. Sweat the details. Go to any length to get it right. Don't let even the smallest thing slide. If it bothers you even a little bit, work on it till it doesn't. Poet Paul Valery said, "A poem is never finished, only abandoned." Be objective. Once you've put some good ideas on paper and had time to polish them to your satisfaction, maybe it's time to cart them around the hallways a little bit, even before you take them to your creative director. You're not looking for consensus here, just a disaster check. This may not be your style, and if you're not comfortable doing this, don't. But it can give you a quick reality check, identify holes that need filling, and point out directions that deserve further exploration. Be objective. Listen to what people have to say about your work. If a couple of people have a problem with something, chances are it's real. Keep in mind that when you're showing an ad around the agency, you're showing it to people who want to like it. Once your ad's out the door, it's quite the opposite. People will approach your ad thinking it's going to be as bad as everything else they see .

So listen to them. There's the old maxim: "When 10 people say you have a tail, sooner or later you oughta turn around and look." Kill off the weak sister. If your campaign has even one weak ad in it, replace that okay ad with one that is as great as the others. I have often talked myself into presenting campaigns that include weak sisters because time was running out. But readers don't care if most of your ads are great. They see them one at a time, so they all should be excellent. There's a saying the Japanese use regarding the strict quality control in their best companies: "How many times a year is it acceptable for the birthing nurse to drop a baby on its head?" Is even one time okay? There's another famous line. I don't know who wrote it. "Good is the enemy of great." It's true. Good is easy to like. Good throws its arm around you and says, "Hey, I'm not so bad, am I?" You talk yourself into it. Next thing you know you have a campaign that goes great—great—good. And that's bad. WHAT TO DO IF YOU'RE STUCK. First of all, being stuck is a good sign. Really. Being stuck means you have moved through all the easy stuff. You've waded through all the crappy ideas, through the okay ideas, passed the low-hanging fruit, and are entering the outlying area of big, new thoughts. Being stuck is not only not unusual, it's what you want. So don't be creeped out by those long silences that can happen during creative sessions. You can spend whole days, even weeks, trying very hard, and come up with diddly. But I've found it's only after you've suffered these excruciating days of meat-loaf brain that the shiny and beautiful finally presents itself to you. The trick is to stay with it. Suffer through it. Remember, the only way out is through. Leave the room and go work somewhere else. A conference room maybe. Or leave the agency. Work in a public place. Some restaurants are close to empty between one and five in the afternoon. Hotel lobbies are great, especially those lobbies on the second floor that looked really "sharp and modern" on the architect's drawing but nobody ever uses. And as Sally Hogshead reminds us, "Domino's delivers to Starbucks." There are other things you can do. If the print isn't coming, work on the radio. If you can't write the headline, write the body copy. And if it's not happening during office hours, stop in the middle of dinner and write. If you are in difficulties with a book, try the element of surprise: attack it at an hour when it isn't expecting it. —H.G. Wells Get off the stinking computer. If your keyboard freezes up, get a pen and paper. In fact, you may find handwriting brings an altogether different part of your brain into play. David Fowler agrees: "Try it. . . . It's just different. The connection between your hand and the page via a tiny strand of ink imparts something that's somehow closer to your heart."5 Ignore the little voice that says,"I'm just a hack on crack from Hackensack." We all feel that way. Even the superstars in this business secretly believe they're hacks at least twice a day. The difference is they get better about ignoring it. In their book Pick Me, Vonk and Kestin give advice on making the evil little voice shut up. You have to learn to mute the voice. Or just use it to spur you on to do better. The painful truth is that all the awards in the world don't take away the tyranny of the blank page. The only thing that does is making a mark on it. Somehow, just getting those first few thoughts out is helpful, even if they genuinely do suck. The act of moving the pen across the paper is the antidote to the belief that you can't do it.6 Go to the store where they sell the stuff. There is demographic data typed neatly on paper. And then there's the stark reality of a customer standing in front of a store shelf looking at your brand and at Brand X. I'm not saying you should start bothering strangers in store aisles with questions. Go ahead if you like. I find it inspiring just to soak in the vibes of the marketplace. Just watch. Think. I guarantee you'll come back with some ideas. Ask your creative director for help. That's what they're there for. There is no dishonor in throwing up your hands and saying, "I'm in a dark and terrible place. Help me or I shall perish." Your CD may be able to see things you can't. She hasn't had her nose two inches away from the problem for the last two weeks like you have. She knows the client, knows the market, and can give you more than an educated guess on what's jamming up your creative process. Sometimes all it takes is a little push, two inches to the left, to get you back on track. Get more product information. You may not know enough about the problem yet, or you may not have enough information on the market. So ask your account folks or planners to go deeper into their files and bring you new stuff. It's likely they edited their pile of information and gleaned what they thought most important. Get to the original material if you can. If you're stuck, relax. Most of the books that I've read on creativity keep bringing up the subject of relaxation. You can't be creative and be tense. The two events are never in the same room together. Stay loose. Breathe from the stomach. If you're not relaxed, stop until you are. Just the simple act of physical relaxation will bring on new ideas. I promise. But remember, you do need a certain amount of pressure to be creative. Creativity rarely happens when things are perfectly under control. To make the kettle boil, a little fire is necessary, and a deadline that's a month and a half away isn't always a good thing. I find that if I have too much time to complete a project, I'll put off working on it until two or three weeks before it's due just so I can dial up the pressure a little bit. The trick is to control the pressure, not let it control you. Relax

Read an old Far Side collection by Gary Larson. The man is an absolute screaming genius. The cartoons are always funny. But look at the economy of his ideas. Look how simple they are. How few moving parts there are. At the very least, with a trip to Larson's sick little world you get a break from the tension. But you might get that small nudge you need. I know I have. I also get that nudge by leafing through magazines from different categories. I'll be working on an insurance campaign, but if there's a snowboarding magazine on the conference room table, I'll pick it up and go through it. Leafing through the awards annuals is okay, too. The shows are a good learning tool, early in the business; they're a good starting point, early in the ideation process. But at some point, they will begin to steer your thinking. (I know plenty of absolutely stellar advertising people who don't own a single CA or One Show.) They realize, sooner or later, they're going to have to unmoor and sail into the unknown. Go to a bookstore and page through books on your subject. Say you're doing an ad on outboard engines. Go to a bookstore and page through books on lakes, oceans, submarines, vacation spots, fish, pistons, hydraulics, whatever. Just let your brain soak up those molecular building blocks of future concepts. You might get the ideas flowing right there in the store.And even if you don't, what's to risk except maybe getting the hairy eyeball from the clerk who thinks you ought to be buying something. ("Hey, whattaya think this is? A li-berry?") Sometimes it's good to work on three projects at once. You may find that the ideas come faster if you move between projects every hour or so. Designer Milton Glaser said, "Working on one thing at a time is like facing a rhinoceros; working on ten things at a time is like playing badminton." Don't burn up too much energy trying to make something work. Follow the first rule of holes: If you are in one, stop digging. There's a book called Lateral Thinking, by Edward DeBono. His metaphor: Don't dig one hole and keep digging down until you hit oil; dig lots of shallow holes first, all over the yard. Even when you do manage to force a decent idea onto paper, after hours of wrestling with it, it usually bears the earmarks of a fight. You can count the dents where you pounded on the poor thing to force it into the shape you wanted. There's none of the spontaneous elegance of an idea born in a moment of illumination. Be patient. Tell yourself it will come. Don't keep swinging at the ball when your arms hurt. Maybe today's not the day. Give up. Go see a movie. Come back tomorrow. Pick up the bat and keep trying. Be patient. Learn to enjoy the process. Not just the finished ad. I used to hate the long process of writing an ad. I simply wanted the reprint in my hands. I wanted to be in L.A. editing the spot. But thinking like this made my job harder than it had to be. The fact is, most of your time in this business will be spent in some cluttered, just-slightly-too-warm room, thinking, not admiring your finished work. Even if you have an award-winning career, only 0.00000002 percent of it will be spent walking up to the podium to accept an award at the One Show. You will spend most of your career trying to decide whether crisp or flaky is the right word to use. Keep reminding yourself: Let the fun be in the chase. Remember you aren't saving lives. When you get stressed and the walls are closing in and you're going nuts trying to crack a problem and you find yourself getting depressed, try to remember that you're just doing an ad. That is all. An ad. A stupid piece of paper. It's not even a whole piece of paper you're working on. It's just a half of a piece of paper in a magazine, and somebody else is buying the other side. Remember, advertising is powerful, and even a "pretty okay" ad can increase sales. (I know, I know. Don't tell my clients I said this. But we're talking those times when it feels like your mental health is at stake.) Don't kill the goose trying to get a golden egg on demand. 110 "Hey, Whipple, Squeeze This" 15934_Sullivan_c04_3p.r.qxp 1/2/08 10:07 AM Page 110 Bertrand Russell said: "One of the symptoms of an approaching nervous breakdown is the belief that one's work is terribly important" INSANITY, OFFICE POLITICS, AND AWARDS SHOWS. "Be orderly in your normal life so you can be violent and original in your work." I don't know much about novelist Gustave Flaubert, except he said the cool line you just read, and it seems to fit in right about here. Many creative people find that a dash of ritual in their lives provides just the structure they need to let go creatively. I happen to prefer an extremely clean and empty room in which to write. That may sound weird, but I've heard of stranger things. In The Art and Science of Creativity, George Kneller wrote: "Schiller [the German poet] filled his desk with rotten apples; Proust worked in a cork-lined room. . . . While [Kant was] writing The Critique of Pure Reason, he would concentrate on a tower visible from his window. When some trees grew up to hide the tower, [he had] authorities cut down the trees so that he could continue his work."7 Your office manager may not like it, but if some trees are bugging you, hack those suckers down. Be buttoned-up. This is a business. The whole chaos-is-good, whiskey-and-cigarettes, showing-up-late-for-work thing is fine for artists and rock stars. But advertising is only half art. It's also half business. The thing is, both halves are on the deadline. So don't be sloppy. Don't be late. Meet your deadlines. Don't lose your writer's headlines. Don't leave your art director's layouts at home. Don't forget to do the outdoor because the print is more fun. This also applies to expense reports and time sheets. Learn how to do them early on, do them impeccably, and turn them in on time. Be a grown-up. Sure, they're boring. But, like watching an episode of The Brady Bunch, if you just sit down and apply yourself, the whole unpleasant thing will be over in a half hour. Write When You Get Work 111 15934_Sullivan_c04_3p.r.qxp 1/2/ 08 10:07 AM Page 111 Don't drink or do drugs. You may think that drinking, smoking pot, or doing coke makes you more creative. I used to think so. I was only fooling myself. I bought into that myth of the tortured creative person, struggling against uncaring clients and blind product managers. With a bottle next to his typewriter and his wastebasket filling ever higher with rejected brilliance, this poor, misunderstood soul constantly looks for that next fantastic idea to rocket him into happiness. In a business where we all try to avoid clichés, a lot of people buy into this cliché-as-lifestyle. I can assure you it is illusion. Identify your most productive working hours and use them for nothing but idea generation. I happen to be a morning person. By three in the afternoon, my brain is meat loaf and a TV campaign featuring a grocer named Whipple doesn't seem like such a bad idea. But you might be sharper in the afternoon. Just strike while your iron is hot. And save those down hours for the busywork of advertising. What I call "phone calls and arguments." Keep your eye on the ball, not on the players. Don't get into office politics. Not all offices have them. If yours does, remember your priority—doing ads. Keep your eye on the ad on your desk. You are a member of a team. Don't ever forget that. Never get into that "I did the visual" or "I did the headline" thing. You work as a team; you lose as a team; you win as a team. You are not genetically superior to account executives. During my first years in the business I was trained to look down on account executives. At the time, it seemed kind of cool to have a bad guy to make fun of. ("Oh, he couldn't sell a joint at Woodstock." "She couldn't sell a compass to Amelia Earhart.") But I was an idiot. 112 "Hey, Whipple, Squeeze This" 15934_Sullivan_c04_3p.r.qxp 1/2/08 10:07 AM Page 112 It's wrong to think that way. They are on my side. Make sure they are on yours. Stay in touch with the real world. Young creative people start out hungry. They're off the street; they know how people think. And their work is great. Then they get successful. They make more and more money, spend their time in restaurants they never dreamed of, fly back and forth between New York and Los Angeles. Pretty soon, the real world isn't people. It's just a bunch of lights off the right side of the plane. You have to stay in touch if you're going to write advertising that works.8 —Jerry Della Femina Stay in touch with the world. Read. Listen. Go places. One of my personal favorites is to watch TV all the time. (Is this a great business or what?) "What are you doing, honey?" "Oh, I'm in here analyzing the psyche of my culture—absorbing the zeitgeist, as it were. I can't be bothered." Read books and magazines. See all the movies. Go to the weird new exhibits at the museums. Know what's out there, good and bad. It's called keeping your finger on the pulse of the culture, all of which has direct bearing on your craft. On the value of awards shows. I shouldn't talk. In my younger days, I was a pathetic awards hound. Just around April, you'd find me lurking in the mail room pining for "the letter" from the One Show announcing accepted entries. "Is it here yet? . . . Well, check againnnnnn." But I won't be too hard on myself. Our work isn't signed. And when you're new in the business, there's no better way to make a name for yourself than getting into "the books. Awards shows allow tiny agencies to compete with the behemoths. They serve as great recruiting tools for agencies. And they expose us to all kinds of work we'd not see otherwise. So I recommend them. With some caveats. Don't make the wrong name for yourself by entering too many campaigns for easy, microscopic, or public service clients. They might get in. Write When You Get Work 113 15934_Sullivan_c04_3p.r.qxp 1/ 2/08 10:07 AM Page 113 Don't talk about awards shows around clients or account executives. You'll devalue yourself in their eyes and make your work suspect.("Is that last ad she did on strategy or is it just another entry into Clever-Fest?") Don't enter every show. As of this writing, I count 39 different national awards shows in this industry. No kidding—39. It's pathetic how much this industry awards itself. (Remember, we aren't saving lives. Even Hollywood isn't this award-crazy.) Thirty-nine, and that's not even counting the local shows. Here's the deal. Only three of them have any merit. In my opinion, the best are the One Show and Communication Arts. And, in England, D&AD. One last thing. If awards are why you want to get into the business, don't get into the business. Awards are candy. They're fun. But by nature of their exclusivity, they represent about 0.000002 percent of all the work being created every year. If you hang your self-esteem on such odds, you're likely to be disappointed. Here's the other thing. If winning awards becomes true north on your compass, you'll warp your understanding of what this business is about: building brands and increasing sales. Yes, I want you to win all kinds of awards by hitting that sweet spot we talked about in Chapter 3—doing ads that are great for your book and great for the client's sales. But when you sit down to work on an ad, make sure you're trying to get into a customer's head and not into the award books. I remember a long, interesting talk with my former boss, Mike Hughes, of The Martin Agency. Over lunch one day, we wondered what it would be like if there were no award shows. Or barring that, what if our respective agencies actually banned creatives from entering their work in them? What would the creative teams come up with if we took away the gravitational pull of the shows? Where would creatives go if all constraints, all presuppositions, and every bit of influence were removed, including the influence of the design and advertising trends being lauded in the latest awards annuals? Our opinion was that the teams would probably start experimenting in some fresh and entirely unexplored areas. As it turns out, neither of us had the guts to stop our agencies from entering work in the award shows. We understood that peer recognition is an important part of any endeavor. Still, we looked at each other and wondered, "What if?"

In the Future, Everyone Will Be Famous for 30 Seconds

SOMEWHERE IN AMERICA IS THE WORST DENTIST; he's out there somewhere. We don't know where he is, but he's out there right now, probably accidentally sticking a novocaine needle in somebody's nose or putting a filling in their dentures. He is the worst dentist in the entire country. And here's the rub: No one knows who he is. That's right. He's the worst dentist in all of America, and he does his horrible work in anonymity. You don't hear people gathered in the company kitchen goin', "Oh, man, did you see that piece of crap bridgework Dr. Hansen did last week? Teeth made outta old paperback books and Bubble Yum? Guy's a complete idiot." On the other hand, where is the worst commercial in all of America? It's right there on national TV, playing night after night. Unlike the anonymity the worst dentist enjoys, our failures here in the ad industry are very public. The worst commercials from the worst agencies (and the worst clients) are all right up there on the big 15934_Sullivan_c05_3p.r.qxp 1/2/08 10:17 AM Page 117 screen, in all their digital horror, seen by tens of millions every night. And people do talk about them at the office. Here's my point: You don't wanna suck in this business of advertising, and you really don't want to suck at TV. Even your mom's gonna see it. People generally get into this business learning their craft on print ads. But you'll find as you grow, you need to start doing more and more TV. To advance, you'll have to do it well. The medium remains a powerful way to sell stuff despite all the inroads made by alternative media like the Internet, digital video recorders, cell phones, DVD players, and video on demand. Many of the suggestions from the chapters on general concepting apply to this medium, the virtues of simplicity being perhaps the most important. Here are a few other things I've learned from my colleagues along the way. CREATING

THE COMMERCIAL. Rule #1 in producing a great TV commercial: First, you must write one. It takes exactly as much work to produce a bad TV spot as a good one. If you have a so-so storyboard approved, you're going to put in the same hours producing it that they put in making Apple's famous "1984" commercial (Figure 5.2). The writer's job on a TV spot doesn't end with coming up with the idea. That's just the beginning of a long process—a process you'll play a part in all along the way. Sell a so-so print idea and at least you'll have the thing out of your hair relatively quickly. A so-so TV spot will haunt you for weeks. You'll have the same long casting sessions as you would producing a great spot, the same boring hours on the set during prelighting, and the same cold coffee in the editing suites. But when you're done, you'll have a ho-hum commercial. Put in the hours now, during the creative process. Make the concept great. Otherwise, you will have a long time to wish you did. Make sure you know what kind of money is available for your project before you start. It's no fun to waste time coming up with a great campaign the client can't afford. So ask your account people to provide a real production estimate. Don't let them tell you the client doesn't really know.That's like walking into a Mercedes dealership and telling the salesperson you "don't really know" how much you have to spend. ("I might have $70,000 . . . I might not. I don't really know.") Typically, production estimates are 10 percent of the total TV buy. Getting this figure is sometimes difficult, but somebody somewhere at the client has a dollar amount in his head, and it's best you find out what it is now. Remember, just because you can think it up doesn't mean you can shoot it. Before you get too excited about selling an idea, make sure your idea can be executed within your budget. Even the simplest effects can be surprisingly expensive, and some are hard to pull off regardless of the money available—particularly if they involve animals, children, or water.

Study the reels. There's nothing like seeing a great commercial on a real television screen. They just don't make the transition to the printed page very well. (That's why I've included only a few stills from favorite spots in this chapter.) You need to see the reels. There are a lot of them out there. There's the annual Cannes reel. There are the reels from the One Show and Communication Arts. You can also get reels from directors and effects houses, and, of course, there's tons of stuff online. Ask your producers to help keep you up on what's new. Stay abreast, too, of who's shooting the hottest music videos.There's a lot of churn in this industry, with new people coming in all the time: independent filmmakers, students out of school, still photographers moving into film. A sharp producer can help keep you up-to-date. Most of the commercials mentioned in this book are viewable online somewhere. With a few prudently chosen search words you should be able to see all the spots (and the web sites) that are covered here. Solve the problem visually. TV is a visual medium, and it begs for visual solutions. Try to avoid verbal approaches. Don't talk at customers. Tell them a story with pictures. Start with images. Stay with images. There is a saying: "The eye will remember what the ear will forget." Remember the last time you tried to tell somebody about a great commercial you'd seen? Did you recite the script? Or paint a picture? Can you make the picture do all the work? Let your TV concept be so visually powerful that a viewer would get it with the sound turned off. This isn't a rule; it doesn't always work. But when it does, it's great. It means you have a very simple, very visual idea. This famous old Maxell audiotape commercial from the 1970s said it all with one image A guy listening to music on a Maxell tape is literally blown away by the fidelity and power of the sound. You could have been vacuuming your living room when this spot came on and you still understood it.

It's okay to think big, too. Even if you've landed a TV job with a sizable budget, your final spot will be better if your idea is simple. When you have a simple idea and a good budget, all the money ends up on the screen, as they say in Hollywood. You can put the production dollars into amplifying an already cool idea instead of depending on money to give your idea some oomph. The ideas behind these two Canneswinning commercials were, on paper, simple. In Wieden Kennedy's famous "Cog" commercial for Honda (Figure 5.5), it's this: "Let's dramatize how well a Honda is built by showing all the parts working together sorta like dominos." The idea might have been charming on a small scale, but the spot was planned as a two-minute commercial using real car parts and without any special effects—it would be one single, long camera pan along a stylized room as parts of an Accord roll, trip, bump, and set each other off in Rube Goldberg fashion. Ultimately, the action ends in front of an assembled vehicle as a voice-over concludes, "Isn't it nice when things just work?" It took five months of design and preproduction before they could even roll film, and then the real test began. Over the course of one hairy week in a Paris studio, the crew did 605 takes. It's likely you can view the spot today on any of a hundred sites that archive incredible advertising. Another Cannes-winning high-production-value spot that comes to mind is one for Guinness Draught beer called "noitulovE" (Figure 5.6). People who enjoy this Irish brew know it takes a bit longer to draw a Guinness beer from the tap; thus, their tagline: "Good things come to those who wait." AMV BBDO's spot sug gests evolution has really just been one long, long wait for a Guinness beer. A trio of guys at a pub drinking Guinness beer takes a journey backward through eons, devolving through cavemen and monkeys, and finally ends up in the primordial muck as three popeyed mudskippers who look like they could use a beer.

The spot could have been smaller in scale and still would have worked. But you could see the money on the screen, and the wow factor was part of the fun as well as the staying power. Yeah, big can be good. But remember, it's the same with commercials as in Hollywood. If you don't have a good story, you don't have a good commercial or a good movie. If you can make the first two seconds of your spot visually unusual, do so. Think about it. Your viewer's watching TV. His eyes are glued to it. The cop shoots the bad guy. The camera closes in. Oh, no! He shot his partner. Fade to black. You now have two seconds to keep the viewer's eyes on the screen before he heads to the kitchen to eat chili out of a can over the sink. Competition with Funyuns and bathroom breaks isn't the only reason to open strong. When you open with something that's inherently interesting or dramatic, you create what George Lowenstein called a "curiosity gap." He says we feel curiosity when there's a gap between what we know and what we want to know, and describes curiosity as an itch. When you set up your spot with something that opens this gap, it creates an itch, and watching the rest of your commercial is the only way to scratch it. As an example, a well-known spot by Jamie Barrett and Mark Wenneker for Saturn automobiles (Figure 5.7) starts with a very curious image: a man running backward out of his garage. It's hard to see that image and not wonder "What's next?" Eventually we understand that the man's just "backing out" of his garage into a world without cars. They illustrated Saturn's value of "People First" by showing a world of human beings on the road without their cars wrapped around them. (The voice-over explains: "When we design our cars, we don't see sheet metal. We see the people who may one day drive them. Introducing the redesigned L, the VUE, and the allnew ION. It's different in a Saturn.") Here on paper, the spot sounds almost simplistic, but it was elegantly shot, set to an understated piano score, and was a thing of beauty.

The most important part of any television advertisement is its conclusion, the last five seconds. That's the part that resolves, explains, summarizes, or excuses the preceding twenty-five seconds. If you're not clear about the last five seconds, you're not clear about anything, because that's where your premise gets pounded home. Try to write the last five seconds first. If you can't, you don't need to write a spot, you need to develop a premise for a spot.1 A television commercial should entertain throughout the entire spot. Avoid a long buildup to an "unexpected" conclusion, or what I call a "waw-waw" ending. (Remember that muted pair of trumpet notes on shows like Leave It to Beaver?) Once you know a commercial's unexpected ending, how many times will you really enjoy watching it? A great spot is a joy to watch from beginning to end, over and over. There's something new to look for in each frame. Please don't take this to mean I'm against surprise in a TV spot— just gimmicky little switcheroos at the back of a spot. Those suck. Real surprise, the gasp you hear when you move a viewer's whole mind-set from one place to another and in doing so, create insight and a fresh new way of seeing—well, that's pretty cool.

A lot of the bigger clients insist on this, saying that identical print and TV executions will give them "synergy." If your print also happens to work as great TV, fine. But if it doesn't, don't let them force you to drag an idea kicking and screaming from one medium into another. All you should promise the client is the campaign will have one voice, one message, across all media—not an unfair request, not an unfulfillable promise. But if your TV sounds like David Letterman and your print reads like the Wall Street Journal, your campaign isn't holding together. Write sparely. Don't carpet your spot with wall-to-wall copy. Leave breathing room. Lots of it. After you've written your script, get out a really big, scary knife. Like the one in Halloween 4. You'll be glad you did, come editing time. You'll find you need space to let those wonderful moments on film just happen by themselves, quietly, without a voice-over jabbering in your ear. Author Sydney Smith suggested, "In composing, as a general rule, run your pen through every other word you have written; you have no idea what vigor it will give to your style." For 15-second spots, write very, very sparely. Ten- or fifteen-second TV spots are a different animal from a 30. You have no time for a slow build. With four to five seconds already set aside for the wrap-up and client logo, you're looking at 10 very skinny seconds to unpack your show, put it on, and hit the showers. So strip your 15-second TV spots down to the bones. And then strip again down to the marrow. Lock off the camera and keep it to one scene if you can. Even two cuts can make a 15 look choppy. I remember a Toyota 15 that was this simple.The camera is locked down on an empty red Toyota parked on a quiet suburban street. Suddenly a barking dog comes rushing down the driveway of the house behind it and careens into the back of the car. Type comes up to silently explain: "Looks Fast." A pause. Then: "The New Celica Action Package."

Avoid showing what you're saying or saying what you're showing. This idea, discussed in print advertising, has a counterpart here in broadcast, with a few twists. You have two tracks of information in a TV spot occurring simultaneously: audio and visual. To some degree, they have to match up. If either track wanders too far afield of the other, viewers will not know which to attend to; they'll lose interest and begin feeling around in the couch for change. On the other hand, you don't want to have the voice-over and video so joined at the hip that viewers hear again what they've already seen on screen. It's better to have one track complete the other, or play off the other, just as you do in print. That 1 1 3 thing works to great effect here in television. The words and the visuals can supply slightly different pieces of information, tracks that viewers can integrate in their heads. Sometimes you can add creative tension between what is seen and what is heard by giving the copy an unexpected tone, perhaps of irony or understatement. For instance, I remember a Reebok spot featuring a popular Dallas Cowboy running back crashing into defensive players. What you heard, though, was the player quietly musing about how football "allows you to meet so many people." TV'S JUST GONNA KEEP GETTING WEIRDER. I hope these few pieces of advice will be enough to help frame your thinking as you begin working in this cool medium. Its high visibility and public forum make it one of the most exciting media you can work in—the most exciting and most public part being, perhaps, the Super Bowl. There's nothing quite like settling in with a group of friends at the big game to see your cool idea along with a billion other people. Things are going to get really interesting when Internet Protocol TV (IPTV) is fully rolled out and in every home. Basically, IPTV is television provided over the Internet. When it arrives, it'll mean the convergence of all things digital in the home: computers, TV sets, digital recorders—pretty much all of it will be on one device and fed through one pipe.

Actually, all the technology exists now, but broadband speeds are going to have to go up and the price come down before IPTV really takes off. Once it does, though, it'll be a new landscape for customers as well as advertisers. The biggest advantage to your clients is that they can customize a TV commercial not just to a zip code, not just to a neighborhood, but to a customer. You know how Amazon.com sometimes sends a message that says, "Hey, Bob, because of your last purchase, we thought these new titles might interest you"? Well, it's now the same thing on TV but with commercials. Say Bob lives in Chicago. And your client is a cruise line out of Miami. Maybe they co-op with the Weather Channel. So when Chicago's temp goes below freezing, Bob gets a commercial extolling the virtues of Caribbean sailing intercut with the frozen silhouette of Chicago's skyline. The spot ends with a special offer for snowbirds freezing their asses off in Chi-town with a cruise price that includes the exact airfare out of Midway. Bob clicks "Select" on his remote, his TV goes from the Weather Channel to Travelocity.com, and he books the trip. Man, it's a new world. When I was a kid, we had three channels. And we liked it.

CHAPTER TEN

But Wait, There's More!

HE DARK AGES PRODUCED A THING called the Iron Maiden—a coffin with spikes on the inside that slowly skewered the victim as its lid was closed. Yet even the Dark Ages—that period of superstitious insanity and violence—never came up with a torture as horrifying as Suzanne Somers telling me about all the great benefits of the ThighMaster. The direct-response TV (DRTV) part of our industry has traditionally produced some of the most horrible blather in the history of television. Richard Simmons and his Deal-A-Meal cards. The old lady in the First Alert spots who said, "I've fallen and I can't get up!" And most recently, the plague of ab workout machines: the Ab-Ripper, the Ab-inator, the Ab-Whatever. George Orwell must've foreseen the state of modern infomercials when he referred to advertising as "the rattling of a stick inside a swill bucket." But here's the deal. The guy who did that ThighMaster thing? He's a multimillionaire. So are Richard Simmons and Ron Popeil. (Popeil sold his company in 2005 for $55 million.) And all those commercials you hate? They sell products by the Mall-of-America load. 15934_Sullivan_c06_3p.r.qxp 1/2/08 10:08 AM Page 131 Given this, it would seem we've come back around to Mr. Whipple and the main question we started with: To be effective, do DRTV spots and infomercials have to suck? I like selling things. I think it's cool. But when I look at the Home Shopping Network and the geeky way they honk that horn when people call in, well, I throw up in my mouth a little bit. (Is it just me?) Yeah, I know they're makin' money hand over fist and the people who own it could buy and sell me a thousand times. But, again, it comes down to this: For me to actually work in this field of DRTV and infomercials, I need to be able to look my kids in the eyes and say, "Yeah, you should see this thing I worked on today. It's pretty cool." So, in spite of evidence to the contrary, I don't believe DRTV spots and infomercials have to suck to be effective. While we're not in the majority, there are some of us who believe

DRTV can do the heavy lifting required of it, and do it without tossing taste, intelligence, and common decency under the treads of capitalism's tanks. Yes, DRTV has some special considerations— rules, if you will—that help yield better results. And results are why your client comes to work every morning. Results are why more and more blue-chip clients are adding DRTV to their marketing mix. Results are why the big agency holding companies are buying up direct-response agencies left and right. But does getting results mean DRTV has to make us feel so urpy? Well, remember the two overlapping circles in Figure 3.3? Pretend for a minute that one circle represents all the rules the DRTV specialists know about how to make the phone ring and the other circle represents Things That Don't Suck. Isn't it possible the two circles could sometimes overlap? Perhaps the best way to begin is by exorcising some of the horrible things associated with this industry. SPRAY-PAINT TOUPEES AND PSYCHIC FRIENDS. The entire DRTV industry was created by entrepreneurs solely for the purpose of selling widgets on TV. None of these gadgets had a brand—or, at least, not a brand with a purpose beyond making money. Things like the Salad Shooter and the ever-creepy GLH (bald-spot spray paint) were created solely to be promoted on TV. Many of these items weren't even manufactured until after the 132 "Hey, Whipple, Squeeze This" 15934_Sullivan_c06_3p.r.qxp 1/2/08 10:08 AM Page 132 infomercials ran and the marketers had the customers lined up. There was simply no brand to protect, build, or polish; it was all about getting people to call now and cough up $19.95 to get an Inside-The-Shell Scrambler. Since the marketers weren't looking for any long-term relationship, they had no scruples about trying every carnival trick in the book. ("Now how much would you pay?") According to an industry magazine,* the top 25 products being sold via DRTV this very month include three male enhancement creams, four weight-loss supplements, two power wheelchairs, and Urine Gone, an odor elimination spray. Not exactly an august lineup of blue-chip clients. God, next they'll be selling lawyers. (They what? They do already? Never mind.) Because of this pedigree, DRTV has remained advertising's mutant stepchild, kept in a box under the basement stairs. Creative people still walk across the street to avoid saying hello. I don't blame them. I ordered copies of the top 20 all-time moneymakers in DRTV, and after some study I can testify that it looks as bad up close as it did from across the street. Most of these infomercials plugged their made-for-TV product into a prefabricated format: the fake talk show format, the fake news show, and fake rallies (where hundreds of supposed brand advocates filled the studio just to cheer on a can of spray-paint hair). I noted an almost complete absence of production values. Every actor was horrible, reading from a transparent sales script, saying things no human being would say. Then there's the wall-to-wall voice-over of the Constantly Talking Man, as well as the nonstop graphics. The overall feeling one gets watching these shows is of being cornered by a salesman in an elevator at a crack convention. They are exhausting. I also note the music, most of which has the cheap synthesized sound that—a friend of a friend tells me—sounds like porn. And finally, DRTV is frequently used to sell products that people are too embarrassed to buy from an actual human being: male enhancement creams, spraypaint hair-in-a-can, psychic friends. Almost every spot I reviewed was dreadful. So it's not surprising that mainstream creatives and good directors avoid DRTV. Its reputation is deserved. The whole category should be torched and rebuilt. But on our way out, let's grab a few of the good things that seem to work, and then set a lighter to the rest.

IF IMAGE = EMOTION,THEN DRTV = REASON. Recently, marketers have begun to use DRTV to sell real mainstream products such as computers and brokerage services; it's no longer all about kitchen widgets. Part of the reason for this surge is that stations charge a lot less to air DRTV. (There are a couple of reasons for this, but suffice it to say that it costs clients a lot less.) The main reason marketers like DRTV isn't cost anyway, but accountability. Clients can track exactly what they're getting for their money. If brand TV is a shotgun, DRTV is a sniper. My friend Richard Apel is a DRTV expert and explained it to me this way: "To use a bad analogy, God in his infinite beneficence lets the sun shine on the just and the unjust alike, right? Which is kinda like brand advertising. But in DRTV, we're not as benevolent. We want the sun to shine only on the just—you know, those exact people most likely to respond to our spot.The unjust?" he concluded with a smile, "They can go to hell." The ability to pinpoint a client's message to just the right audience and then to track that data in nearly real time has incredible marketing power.Today, customer data is easier, cheaper, and faster than ever to obtain and analyze. My buddy Richard says, "Once clients have had the taste of raw, segmented or analyzed response data, I swear, it becomes like an addiction." Because of this power, DRTV has started to move from latenight into the more respectable hours of daytime and prime-time TV. Along the way, the discipline has attracted lots of blue-chip companies like Apple and Nokia. These are companies that want a revenue-building vehicle like DRTV in their portfolio but aren't willing to cheapen the brand just to make a sale. These brands continue their regular image advertising, which helps give customers a certain feeling about their brand, and then use DRTV to make them act on those feelings. Brand provides the air cover; the troops of retail and direct response do the rest. DRTV takes several forms. Any ad with a consumer response that can be specifically tracked is technically DRTV, but for our purposes we're talking about long form and short form. Long form is any commercial longer than two minutes (the infamous infomercial), and the short form, anything two minutes or under. My friend Jim Warren is a specialist in direct-response TV and he sees DRTV existing along a spectrum (Figure 6.2). On one side 134 "Hey, Whipple, Squeeze This" 15934_Sullivan_c06_3p.r.qxp 1/2/08 10:08 AM Page 134 there's pure brand advertising; on the other is hard-core DRTV. But, he continues, ROI and accountability pressures are requiring agencies to move away from both extremes and instead find sweet spots along the spectrum that satisfy both of the objectives most important to their clients: 1) building a brand that people love, and 2) selling the products to those people. In other words, all advertisements should have at least some of both components, and there's only limited reason for ads on the extreme ends of the brand-demand spectrum.1 Here's another way to think of the brand-to-direct spectrum. (It's creepy, but bear with me.) If image advertising is kinda like a first date, DRTV is the second. On a second date, you're done trying to get someone's attention, right? You have it, obviously. They seem to like you and now they just wanna know more about you. Your relationship with the customer has moved from catching their eye from across the room to having a nice, long conversation. It's moved from a chemistry check to looking for rational reasons to buy. (And get married.) Okay, enough with the creepy metaphor. The point is, DRTV is all about providing information, and lots of it. This is your opportunity to remove any objection that could keep a customer from buying your product. It means answering all the questions customers might ask if they were standing in front of you. "The more you tell, the more you sell," says my friend Jim, and if he tells me one more time, I'm gonna barf. But the guy's right. Let's go back to that brand-demand spectrum again. On the left side, it's pure brand image stuff. Cool, we've covered that in Chapter 5. On the right is DRTV, purely expository and full of facts. (And way over on the right is the hard-sell "Call right But Wait, There's More! 135 Figure 6.2 On the left, pure image advertising. In the middle, a little of both. And on the right, pure transaction. 15934_Sullivan_c06_3p.r.qxp 1/ 2/08 10:08 AM Page 135 now!" kind of spot—the kind this book will not touch, even with Ronco's new Ten-Foot Pole®. ("The new Ten-Foot Pole® lets you touch all kinds of skeevy stuff with no muss, no fuss!!") But in between those two extremes, there's a variety of hybrids that allow an advertiser to dial up or down the amount of information and the call to action. With creatives on the general advertising side, the most popular is the lead generation format, which is usually in the shape of a "25/5." It's more on the brand side of the spectrum because here you have 25 seconds of what amounts to brand image advertising followed up with a 5-second call to action. The brilliant GEICO campaign is a perfect example. In the first 25 seconds, GEICO says that it's so easy to lower the cost of your car insurance "even a caveman could do it." (At which point we see modern, well-dressed Neanderthals taking offense at the insult.) The spots all end with a simple call to action: With the phone number up on the screen, the voice-over says, "Fifteen minutes could save you 15 percent on your car insurance." Lead generation spots like this don't need to answer all of a customer's questions, only enough to get them to call. And in GEICO's case, the calls came in. According to Mike Hughes at The Martin Agency, the long-running caveman series is one of GEICO's biggest successes. Now, as we push farther to the right on the spectrum, we dial up the amount of information. Typically, as the amount of information goes up, you move from buying 30-second spots to 60s, and even two-minute spots. It's here where the challenge lies. The more you tell may well mean the more you sell, but it could also mean the more you suck—if you don't find a graceful and intelligent way of telling your story. SHORT- AND LONG-FORM DRTV. Short-form DRTV works best for products that sell themselves quickly because they can be explained in under a minute or two. GEICO's lead generation is a good example of a quick get. But let's say you have a bit more of a story to tell. Well, here's where DRTV differs somewhat from brand image work. You've got a lot of information to impart. You need to present it in a way that makes sense and doesn't bore people.